At Home
In the Smokies

A History Handbook for
Great Smoky Mountains National Park
North Carolina and Tennessee

Produced by the
Division of Publications
National Park Service

U.S. Department of the Interior
Washington, D.C. 1984

Using This Handbook
This theme handbook, published in this new edition
on the 50th anniversary of Great Smoky Mountains
National Park, tells the story of the people who settled and lived in the mountains along the Tennessee
and North Carolina border. Part 1 gives a brief intro-
duction to the park and its historical sites. In Part 2,
Wilma Dykeman and Jim Stokely present the history
of the region from the early Cherokee days to the
establishment of the park in 1934 and the renewed
interest in the past in the 1970s; this text was first
published by the National Park Service in 1978. Part 3
gives a brief description of the major historical buildings you can see in the park. For general information
about the park and its wildlife, see Handbook 112.

National Park Handbooks, compact introductions to
the great natural and historic places administered
by the National Park Service, are published to support
the National Park Service's management programs
at the parks and to promote understanding and enjoyment of the parks. This is Handbook 125.

Library of Congress Cataloging in Publication Data
Main entry under title: At home in the Smokies.
(National park handbook; 125)
Rev. ed. of: Highland homeland/Wilma Dykeman
and Jim Stokely. 1978. Includes index.
Supt. of Docs. no.: I 29.9/5:125
1. Great Smoky Mountains (N.C. and Tenn.)—Social
life and customs. 2. Great Smoky Mountains (N.C.
and Tenn.)—History. 3. Great Smoky Mountains
National Park (N.C. and Tenn.)—Guide-books. 4.
Cherokee Indians—History.
I. Dykeman, Wilma. Highland homeland. II. United
States. National Park Service. Division of Publica-
tions. III. Series: Handbook (United States. National
Park Service. Division of Publications); 125.
F443.G7A8   1984   976.8'89   84-600108
ISBN 0-912627-22-0

Part 1

Recapturing the Past

*Aden Carver of Oconaluftee
was a carpenter, stone
mason, millwright, deacon,
and preacher. He was more
versatile than some men but
representative of many who
worked hard and enjoyed
their lives in the Smokies.*

Smoky Mountain Heritage

Seemingly endless ridges, forests, mountain streams, waterfalls, and wildlife attract hundreds of thousands of travelers each year to Great Smoky Mountains National Park on the Tennessee – North Carolina border. Many are drawn by a long procession of wildflowers and shrubs bursting into bloom in the spring and by the colorful foliage of the hardwoods in the fall. Thousands hike the park's many trails, which range from short spurs to the 110 kilometers (70 miles) of the Appalachian Trail that runs through the park. Also attracting wide interest are the park's historical sites and the lifeways of the mountain people. They are pleasant surprises in the midst of all of nature's richness. They are physical ties with our ancestors, many of whom traveled from their homelands across the sea to build new homes in the relatively unexplored continent of North America.

The National Park Service has preserved some of the historic structures in Great Smoky Mountains National Park so that we, and future generations, can better understand how our forefathers lived. By walking through and closely examining their finely crafted—and crudely crafted—log houses, barns, and other farm buildings we gain a new respect for their diligence and perseverance. The hours spent hewing massive beams, preserving foods for winter use, and making clothes from scratch are nearly incomprehensible in our age of machines and computers. The mountainous terrain demanded hard work, and the isolation fostered a zealous independence. The land truly molded a resourcefulness and hardiness in the Smokies character.

The story of these mountain people and communities is told in Part 2 of this handbook by Wilma Dykeman and Jim Stokely, who can look out on the expanse of the Great Smokies from their family home in Newport, Tennessee. Their engaging story of the Smokies is illustrated with historic photographs that largely come from the park's files. Although the identities of many of the photographers are unknown (see page 160), we are no less indebted to them. They have helped to preserve the history and folkways of the Great Smokies people, who played a part in molding and defining our national character.

In the old days, housekeeping in the Smokies allowed few if any frills. Aunt Rhodie Abbott, and most other women, worked as hard as any man as they went about their daily chores keeping their families fed and clothed.

Part 2

Highland Homeland

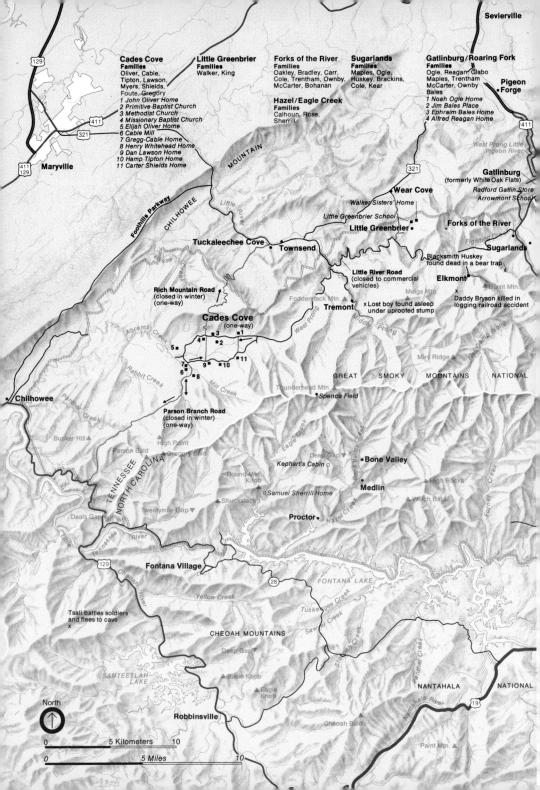

mated to be 500-600 million years old—and its tall peaks and plunging valleys have been sculpted by nature through the action of ice and water during long, patient centuries. The odd and fantastic courses of the rivers here indicate that they are older than the mountains. The Great Smokies are a land of moving waters; there is no natural lake or pond in this area, but there are some 1,000 kilometers (620 miles) of streams with more than 70 species of fish. A generous rainfall, averaging as much as 229 centimeters (90 inches) per year in some localities and 211 centimeters (83 inches) atop Clingmans Dome, nourishes a rich variety of plantlife: more than 100 species of trees, 1,200 other flowering plants, 50 types of fern, 500 mosses and lichens, and 2,000 fungi. The mixed hardwood forest and virgin stands of balsam and spruce are the special glories of the Smokies.

Many of the species of birds that make the Smokies their home do not have to leave to migrate; by migrating vertically, from the valleys to the mountaintops in summer and back down in winter, they can experience the equivalent of a journey at sea level from Georgia to New England. Animals large and small find this a congenial home, and two, the wild boar and the black bear, are especially interesting to visitors. The former shuns people, but the latter is occasionally seen along trails and roadsides throughout the Smokies.

When the Great Smoky Mountains were added to the National Park System in 1934, a unique mission was accomplished: more than 6,600 separate tracts of land had been purchased by the citizens of Tennessee and North Carolina and given to the people of the United States. Previously, most national parks had been created from lands held by the Federal Government. The story of the Great Smokies is, therefore, most especially and significantly, a story of people and their home. Part of that story is captured in microcosm on an August Sunday in a secluded northeastern corner of the park: Cataloochee.

History is what the homecoming is about. The people of Cataloochee worship and sing and eat and celebrate because they are back. And being back, they remember. They walk up the narrow creeks, banked by thick tangles of rhododendron and doghobble, to the sites of old homesteads. They watch

Homecoming

It is summer now, a time for coming home. And on an August Sunday in the mountain-green valley they call Cataloochee, the kinfolk arrive. They come from 50 states to gather here, at a one-room white frame Methodist church by the banks of the Big "Catalooch." The appearance of their shiny cars and bulky campers rolling along the paved Park Service road suggests that they are tourists, too, a tiny part of the millions who visit and enjoy the Great Smoky Mountains each year. Yet these particular families represent something more. A few of them were raised here; their ancestors lived and died here.

They are celebrating their annual Cataloochee homecoming. Other reunions, held on Sundays throughout the summer, bring together onetime residents of almost every area in the park. Some of the places instantly recall bits of history: Greenbrier, once a heavily populated cove and political nerve-center; Elkmont, where a blacksmith named Huskey set out one winter to cross the Smokies and was discovered dead in a bear trap the next spring; and Smokemont on the beautiful Oconaluftee River, at one time the home of the Middle Cherokee and the very heart of that Indian Nation.

These are special days, but they observe a universal experience as old as Homer's Ulysses, as new as the astronauts' return from the moon: homecoming. It is an experience particularly signifcant in the Great Smoky Mountains National Park. Here, at different times and in different ways, people of various races and heritage have reluctantly given up hearth and farm so that today new generations can come to this green kingdom of some 209,000 hectares (517,000 acres) and rediscover a natural homeland which is the heritage of all.

Beginning on Canada's Gaspé Peninsula as a limestone finger only 2.5 kilometers (1.5 miles) wide, the Appalachian mountain system that dominates eastern America slants about 5,000 kilometers (3,000 miles) southwest across New England and the Atlantic and border states into northern Georgia and Alabama, culminating in the grandeur and complexity of the Great Smoky Mountains. This range, which marks the dividing line between Tennessee and North Carolina, is high; its 58-kilometer (36-mile) crest remains more than 1,500 meters (4,900 feet) above sea level. It is ancient—the Ocoee rocks here are esti-

A home in the Smokies usually meant a simple log house nestled in the hills among the trees and amidst the haze.

Big Greenbrier
Families
Whaley, Ownby, Proffitt, Bohanan, Huskey, McCarter, Parton, Green, Price

Forney Creek
Families
Cole, Monteith, Crisp, Welch

Oconaluftee
Families
Mingus, Enloe Hughes, Conner Collins, Beck Bradley, Sherrill Floyd, Carver, Queen

Deep Creek
Families
Wiggins, Beck, Jenkins, Laney, Bumgarner

Cosby
Families
Ramsey, Sutton Webb, Shults

Foothills Parkway
(closed in winter)

Crestmont
Families
Gunter, Webb McGaha, Sutton

CHEROKEE NATIONAL FOREST

Cataloochee
Families
Caldwell, Woody Bennett, Messer, Palmer, Hannah
1 Jarvis Palmer Home
2 Palmer Chapel
3 Beech Grove School
4 Hiram Caldwell Home
5 Steve Woody Home

32

321

Pittman Center

Mt. Cammerer

Crestmont

Big Greenbrier

Little Pigeon River

TENNESSEE

NORTH CAROLINA

big Creek

Cosby Knob

Walnut Bottom

Pigeon River

4
3 2
1

Roaring Fork
Motor Nature Trail
(one-way)

Cherokee Orchard

Dudley Creek

Le Conte Creek

Granny's College

Ramsay Prong

Mt. Guyot

Mt. Chapman

Mt. Sequoyah

Pretty Hollow Gap

Mt. Sterling

Mt. Sterling Gap

Fiddler Grooms slain after playing tune

Jim Hannah Cabin

Ola Post Office

Little Cataloochee Baptist Church

Big Cataloochee Mtn.

Noland Mtn.

40

Bull Head

Alum Cave

Charles Bunion

Straight Fork

Big Cataloochee
1 x Sheriff's assailant hides for years
3 2
George Palmer Home
Levi Caldwell Home
5 4
Nellie Post Office

Mt. Le Conte

Mt. Kephart

Chimney Tops

Mt. Mingus

Sugarland Mtn.

Newfound Gap

Newfound Gap Road
(closed to commercial vehicles)

Indian Gap

Meigs Post

Mt. Collins

PARK

Clingmans Dome

Rattlesnake Knob

Roundtop Knob

Andrews Bald

Buckhorn Bald

Bradley Fork

Long Fork

Caldwell Fork

Rough Fork

Milas Messer Home

276

Big Cove

Round Bottom Road
(closed in winter)
(one-way)

Smokemont

Aden Carver Home

Big Cove Road

Little Bald Knob

Leatherwood Top

Dellwood

Oconaluftee

Mingus Mill

Pioneer Farmstead

Barnett Knob

Bunches Creek

Soco Bald

Jonathans

Maggie

Ravensford

CHEROKEE

Yellowhill

INDIAN

Wiggins Creek

RESERVATION

19

Waynesville

Cherokee

Painttown

Birdtown

Soco Creek

Soco Valley

Blue

Sharp Top

Deep Creek

441

Wolftown

Quallatown

Carter Top

Ridge

Parkway

23

US 19

Bryson City

Ela

Whittier

Oconaluftee River

Connelly Creek

Deep Creek

Noland Creek

Indian Creek

Cooper Creek

Tuckasegee River

Cedar Cliff

Dicks Creek

Scott Creek

Doubletop Mtn.

28

FOREST

Soapstone Knob

Cowee Bald

Alarka Creek

Dilisboro

Sylva

23
441

Moses Creek

Judaculla Rock

Unpaved road	■ Historic building	▲ Peak
	□ Historic building site	⌣ Gap

their small children and grandchildren wade the water and trample the grass of once-familiar fields. They call themselves Caldwell, Palmer, Hannah, Woody, Bennett, Messer. For exactly a century—from the late 1830s and the coming of the first permanent white settlers to the later 1930s and the coming of the park—men and women with these names lived along Cataloochee Creek. But these pioneers were not the first to inhabit a valley that they called by an Indian name.

By "Gad-a-lu-tsi," the Cherokees meant "standing up in ranks." As they looked from Cove Creek Gap at the eastern end of the valley across toward the Balsam Mountains, they used that term to describe the thin stand of timber at the top of the distant range. Later, the name became "Cataloochee," or the colloquial "Catalooch," and it referred to the entire watershed of the central stream.

With their trusty mule and sourwood sled, Giles and Lenard Ownby haul wood for making shingles.

The Cherokees liked what they saw. They hunted and fished throughout the area and established small villages along one of their main trails. The Cataloochee Track, as it came to be known, ran from Cove Creek Gap at the eastern edge of the present-day park up over the Smokies and down through what is now the Cosby section of eastern Tennessee. It connected large Indian settlements along the upper French Broad River in North Carolina with the equally important Overhill Towns of the Tennessee River.

By the early 1700s, Cataloochee formed a minor portion of the great Cherokee Nation whose towns and villages extended from eastern Tennessee and western North Carolina into northern Georgia. But as time went on, and as the white settlements pushed westward from the wide eastern front, the Cherokees lost dominion over this vast area. In 1791, at the treaty of Holston, the Cherokees gave up Cataloochee along with much of what is now East Tennessee. Five years later the state of North Carolina granted 71,210 hectares (176,000 acres), including all of Cataloochee, to John Gray Blount—brother to William Blount, governor of the Territory South of the Ohio River, as Tennessee was then called. Blount kept the land for speculation, but it eventually sold for less than one cent per hectare. Now that the Cherokees had relinquished the land, no one else seemed to want it. Even the famous Methodist Bishop Francis Asbury, first sent as a missionary to America in 1771, apparently wavered in his spirit when confronted with the Cataloochee wilderness. In his journal in 1810 he lamented:

"At Catahouche I walked over a log. But O the mountain height after height, and five miles over! After crossing other streams, and losing ourselves in the woods, we came in, about nine o'clock at night. . . . What an awful day!"

During the 1820s, only a few hunters, trappers, and fishermen built overnight cabins in the area. Then in 1834, Col. Robert Love, who had migrated from Virginia, fought in the Revolutionary War, and established a farm near the present city of Asheville, purchased the original Blount tract for $3,000. To keep title to the land, Love was required to maintain permanent settlers there. He encouraged cattle ranging and permitted settlers choice locations and unlimited terms, and by the late 1830s several families had moved into Cataloochee. Probably the first settler to put down roots was young Levi Caldwell, a householder in his early twenties seeking a good home for his new family. The rich bottomlands and abundant forests of Cataloochee offered that home, and before Levi Caldwell died in 1864 at the age of 49, he and his wife "Polly" (Mary Nailling) had 11 children. Levi was a prisoner during the Civil War, and two of his sons, Andrew and William Harrison, fought on different sides. Because he had tended horses for the widely feared band of Union soldiers called Kirk's Army, Andy received a $12 pension when the war was over. William, who might have forgiven and forgotten his differences with the Union as a whole, was never quite reconciled to his brother's pension.

Although he was older than Levi Caldwell by a full 21 years, George Palmer arrived later at Catalooch. The Palmers had settled further northeast in the North Carolina mountains, on Sandy Mush Creek, and seemed content there. But when George decided to start over, he and his wife, also named Polly, took their youngest children, Jesse and George Lafayette, and crossed the mountains south into Cataloochee. They began again.

Other families trickled in. As elsewhere in Southern Appalachia, buffalo traces and old Indian trails and more recent traders' paths gradually became roads and highways penetrating the thick forests and mountain fastnesses. In 1846, the North Carolina legislature passed an act creating the Jonathan Creek and Tennessee Mountain Turnpike Company, which was to build a road no less than 3.7 meters (12 feet) wide and no steeper than a 12 percent grade. Tolls would range from 75 cents for a six-horse wagon down to a dime for a man or a horse and one cent for each hog or sheep. After a full five years of deliberation and examining alternatives, the company selected a final route and constructed the highway with minor difficulty. The road fully utilized the natural contours of the land and was at the same time a generally direct line. It followed almost exactly the old Cherokee Trail.

The Cataloochee Turnpike was the first real wagon road in the Smokies. It opened up a chink in the area's armor of isolation. Travel to and from the county seat still required the better part of three days, however. Two of the rare 19th century literary visitors to these mountains—Wilbur Zeigler and Ben Grosscup, whose book *The Heart of the Alleghanies,* appeared in 1883—entered Cataloochee along this road. Their reaction provides a pleasant contrast to that of Bishop Asbury; they speak of the "canon of the Cataluche" as being "the most picturesque valley of the Great Smoky range:"

"The mountains are timbered, but precipitous; the narrow, level lands between are fertile; farm houses look upon a rambling road, and a creek, noted as a prolific trout stream, runs a devious course through hemlock forests, around romantic cliffs, and between laureled banks."

During the 1840s and 1850s, some 15 or 20 families built their sturdy log cabins ax-hewn out of huge chestnuts and poplars, and then built barns, smokehouses, corncribs, and other farm shelters beside the rocky creeks. George Palmer's son Lafayette, called "Fate" for short, married one of Levi Caldwell's daughters and established a large homestead by the main stream. Fate's brother, Jesse, married and had 13 children; 6 of these 13 later married Caldwells.

They ate well. The creek bottomlands provided rich soil for tomatoes, corn and beans, cabbage and onions, potatoes and pumpkins. Split rail fences were devices to keep the cattle, hogs, and sheep out of the crops; the animals themselves foraged freely through-

Cataloochee and Caldwell—the names are nearly synonymous. The Lush Caldwell family once lived in this sturdy log house with shake roof and stone chimneys on Messer Fork. At another time, this was the home of the E. J. Messers, another of Cataloochee's predominant families.

Pages 22-23: These proud people all dressed up in their Sunday best are members of the George H. Caldwell family.

21

out the watershed, fattening on succulent grasses and an ample mast of acorns and chestnuts. Corn filled the cribs, salted pork and beef layered the meathouse, and cold bountiful springs watered the valley.

The Civil War erupted in 1861. Although Cataloochee lay officially in the Confederacy, this creek country was so remote, so distant from the slave plantations of the deep South, that no government dominated. Raiding parties from both sides rode through the valley, killing and looting as they went. Near Mt. Sterling Gap at the northern end of the watershed, Kirk's Army made a man named Grooms play a fiddle before they murdered him. The people of Cataloch kept his memory alive throughout the century by playing that ill-starred "Grooms tune."

But the war was only an interlude. Five years after its end, Cataloochee was estimated to have 500 hogs, sheep, milch cows, beef cattle, and horses; some 900 kilograms (2,000 pounds) of honey; and about 1,250 liters (1,320 quarts) of sorghum molasses. Sizable apple crops would begin to flourish during the next decade, and by 1900 the population of the valley would grow to over 700. Producing more than they themselves could use, these farmers began to trade with the outside world. They took their apples, livestock, chestnuts, eggs, honey, and ginseng to North Carolina markets in Fines Creek, Canton, and Waynesville, and to Tennessee outlets in Cosby, Newport, and Knoxville. With their cash money, they changed forever the Cataloochee of the early 1800s.

They sold honey and bought the tools of education. Using the tough, straight wood of a black gum or a basswood, a farmer hollowed out a section of the trunk with a chisel. He then slid a cross-stick through a hole bored near the bottom. Upon transplanting a beehive into the trunk and leaving an entrance at the bottom, he covered the top with a solid wooden lid and sealed it airtight with a mixture of mud and swamp-clay. In August, especially after the sourwoods had bloomed and the bees had built up a store of the delicately flavored honey, the bee-keeper took a long hooked honey knife, broke the sealing, and cut out squares of the light golden comb to fill ten-gallon tins. He never went below the cross-stick; that honey was left for the bees. An enterpris-

ing family might trade 10 tins of honey in a season. And at the market, they would turn that honey into school supplies for the coming year: shoes, books, tablets, and pencils.

There were too few families on Big Cataloochee for both a Methodist and a Baptist church. In 1858 Colonel Love's son had deeded a small tract there for the Palmers, Bennetts, Caldwells, and Woodys to use as a Methodist meetinghouse and school. Since then, the Messers and Hannahs and several others had formed a community of their own 8 kilometers (5 miles) north, across Noland Mountain, along the smaller valley of the Little Cataloochee. They built a Baptist church there in 1890.

But the differences were not great. One of the Big Cataloochee's sons became and remained the high sheriff of sprawling Haywood County with the well-nigh solid support of the combined Cataloochee vote. Running six times in succession and against a candidate from the southeastern part of the county, he was rumored to have waited each time for the more accessible lowlands to record their early returns. Then he simply contacted a cousin, who happened to be the recorder for Cataloochee, who would ask in his slow, easy voice, "How many do you need, cousin?"

The preacher came once a month. He stayed with different families in the community and met the rest at church. More informal gatherings, such as Sunday School and singings, took place each week. And during late summer or fall, when crops were "laid by" and there was an interval between spring's cultivation and autumn's harvest, there came the socializing and fervor of camp meeting. A one-week or ten-day revival was cause for school to be let out at 11 o'clock each morning. The children were required to attend long and fervent services. But between exhortations there were feasts of food, frolicking in nearby fields and streams, and for everyone an exchange of good fellowship.

Besides these religious gatherings, women held bean-stringings and quilting bees, men assembled for logrollings or house-raisings to clear new lands and build new homes. One of the few governmental intrusions into Cataloochee life was the road requirement. During the spring and fall, all able-bodied men were "warned out" for six days—eight if there had been

washout rains—to keep up what had become the well-used Cataloochee Turnpike. If a man brought a mule and a bull-tongue plow instead of the usual mattock, he received double time for ditching the sides of the road. This heavy work gave the men both a chance to talk and something to talk about. But any of them would still have said that the hardest job of the year was hoeing corn all day on a lonely, stony hillside.

By the early 1900s, Cataloochee had become a mixture of isolation from the outside world and communication with it. Outside laws had affected the valley; in 1885 North Carolina passed the controversial No Fence law, which made fences within townships unnecessary and required owners to keep cattle, sheep, horses, and hogs inside certain bounds. But other laws were less heeded; local experts have estimated that 95 percent of Cataloochee residents made their own whisky. Several families subscribed to a newspaper—"Uncle Jim" Woody took *The Atlanta Constitution*—and almost everyone possessed the "wish-book:" a dog-eared mail order catalog. But no one in Little Cataloochee bought an automobile.

The valley thrived on local incidents. A man shot a deputy sheriff and hid out near a large rock above Fate Palmer's homestead; Neddy McFalls and Dick Clark fed him there for years. Will Messer, a master carpenter and coffinmaker over on Little Cataloch, had a daughter named Ola. Messer was postmaster, and the post office acquired her name. Fate Palmer's shy son, Robert, became known as the "Booger Man" after he hid his face in his arms and gave that as his name to a new teacher on the first day of school.

George Palmer, son of Jesse and brother to Sheriff William, devised a method of capturing wild turkeys. He first built a log enclosure, then dug a trench under one side and baited it with corn. The next morning 10 turkeys, too frightened to retrace their steps through the trench, showed up inside the enclosure. But when George stepped among them and attempted to catch them, the turkeys gave him the beating of his life. Thereafter he was called "Turkey George." And his daughter, Nellie, lent her name to one of the two post offices on Big Cataloch.

Yet the simplicity of life could not insulate the Cataloochee area from "progress." As the 20th cen-

Like many others in the Smokies, Dan Myers of Cades Cove kept a few bees. He apparently was a little more carefree than some about the tops of his bee gums, or hives. Some old boards or scraps of tin, with the help of a couple of rocks, sufficed, whereas most people sealed their wooden tops with a little mud.

Charles S. Grossman

27

washout rains—to keep up what had become the well-used Cataloochee Turnpike. If a man brought a mule and a bull-tongue plow instead of the usual mattock, he received double time for ditching the sides of the road. This heavy work gave the men both a chance to talk and something to talk about. But any of them would still have said that the hardest job of the year was hoeing corn all day on a lonely, stony hillside.

By the early 1900s, Cataloochee had become a mixture of isolation from the outside world and communication with it. Outside laws had affected the valley; in 1885 North Carolina passed the controversial No Fence law, which made fences within townships unnecessary and required owners to keep cattle, sheep, horses, and hogs inside certain bounds. But other laws were less heeded; local experts have estimated that 95 percent of Cataloochee residents made their own whisky. Several families subscribed to a newspaper—"Uncle Jim" Woody took *The Atlanta Constitution*—and almost everyone possessed the "wish-book:" a dog-eared mail order catalog. But no one in Little Cataloochee bought an automobile.

The valley thrived on local incidents. A man shot a deputy sheriff and hid out near a large rock above Fate Palmer's homestead; Neddy McFalls and Dick Clark fed him there for years. Will Messer, a master carpenter and coffinmaker over on Little Catalooch, had a daughter named Ola. Messer was postmaster, and the post office acquired her name. Fate Palmer's shy son, Robert, became known as the "Booger Man" after he hid his face in his arms and gave that as his name to a new teacher on the first day of school.

George Palmer, son of Jesse and brother to Sheriff William, devised a method of capturing wild turkeys. He first built a log enclosure, then dug a trench under one side and baited it with corn. The next morning 10 turkeys, too frightened to retrace their steps through the trench, showed up inside the enclosure. But when George stepped among them and attempted to catch them, the turkeys gave him the beating of his life. Thereafter he was called "Turkey George." And his daughter, Nellie, lent her name to one of the two post offices on Big Catalooch.

Yet the simplicity of life could not insulate the Cataloochee area from "progress." As the 20th cen-

Like many others in the Smokies, Dan Myers of Cades Cove kept a few bees. He apparently was a little more carefree than some about the tops of his bee gums, or hives. Some old boards or scraps of tin, with the help of a couple of rocks, sufficed, whereas most people sealed their wooden tops with a little mud.

Charles S. Grossman

27

tury unfolded, scattered individual loggers gave way to the well organized methods of large company operations. Small-scale cutting of yellow-tulip poplar and cherry boomed into big business during the early 1900s. Suncrest Lumber Company, with a sawmill in Waynesville, began operations on Cataloochee Creek and hauled out hardwood logs in great quantities. Although the spruce and balsam at the head of the watershed were left standing, the logging industry, with its capital, manpower, and influence, vastly altered the valley.

With the late 1920s came an announcement that the states of North Carolina and Tennessee had decided to give the Great Smoky Mountains to the nation as a park. The residents of Cataloochee were incredulous. They were attached to this homeplace; they still referred to a short wagon ride as a trip and called a visit to the county seat a journey. But the park arrived, and the young families of the valley moved away, and then the older ones did the same. Gradually they came to understand that another sort of homeland had been established. And the strangers who now visit their valleys and creeks can look about and appreciate the heritage these settlers and their descendants left behind.

The old families still come back. They return to this creek on the August Sunday of Homecoming. In the early morning hours they fill the wooden benches of tiny Palmer's Chapel for singing and preaching and reminiscing; at noon they share bountiful food spread on long plank tables beside clear, rushing Cataloochee Creek; in the mellow afternoon they rediscover the valley. For what lures the stranger is what lures the old families back. They come to sense again the beauty and the permanence and even the foggy mystery of the Great Smokies. And this that beckons them back is that which beckoned the Indian discoverers of these mountains hundreds of years ago.

"Turkey George" Palmer of Pretty Hollow Creek in Cataloochee used to tell people that he had killed 105 bears. Most of them he trapped in bear pens.

Edouard E. Exline

Rail Fences

"Something there is that does not love a wall," poet Robert Frost once wrote. Likewise, many mountain people felt something there is that does not love a fence. Fences were built for the purpose of keeping certain creatures out —and keeping other creatures in. During early days of settlement there were no stock-laws in the mountains. Cattle, mules, horses, hogs, sheep, and fowls ranged freely over the countryside. Each farmer had to build fences to protect his garden and crops from these domestic foragers as well as some of the wild "varmint" marauders. Rail fences had several distinct merits: they provided a practical use for some of the trees felled to clear crop and pasture land; they required little repair; they blended esthetically into the surroundings and landscape. Mountain fences have been described as "horse-high, bull-strong, and pig-tight." W. Clark Medford, of North Carolina, has told us how worm fences (right) were built:

"There was no way to build a fence in those days except

H. Woodbridge Williams

with rails—just like there was no way to cover a house except with boards. First, they went into the woods, cut a good 'rail tree' and, with axes, wedge and gluts, split the cuts (of six-, eight- and ten-foot lengths as desired) into the rail. After being hauled to location, they were placed along the fence-way, which had already been cut out and made ready. Next, the 'worm' was laid. That is, the ground-rails were put down, end-on-end, alternating the lengths—first a long rail, then a short one—and so on through. Any-one who has seen a rail fence knows that the rails were laid end-on-end at angles—not at right angles, but nearly so. One course of rails after another would be laid up on the fence until it had reached the desired height (most fences were about eight rails high, some ten). Then, at intervals, the corners (where the rails lapped) would be propped with poles, and sometimes a stake would be driven. Such fences, when built of good chestnut or chestnut-oak rails, lasted for many years if kept from falling down."

One of the most valuable fences ever constructed in the Smoky Mountains was surely that of Abraham Mingus. When "Uncle Abe," one-time postmaster and miller, needed rails for fencing, he "cut into a field thick with walnut timber, split the tree bodies, and fenced his land with black walnut rails." The variety of fences was nearly infinite. Sherman Myers leans against a sturdy post and rider (below) near Primitive Baptist Church. Other kinds of fences are shown on the next two pages.

In this post and rider variation, rails are fastened to a single post with wire and staples.

Mary Birchfield of Cades Cove had an unusual fence with wire wound around crude pickets.

In the summer, farmers enclosed haystacks to keep grazing cattle away.

Ki Cable's worm, or snake, fence in Cades Cove is one of the most common kinds of fencing.

Poles were used at John Oliver's Cades Cove farm to line up the wall as it was built.

Land of the Cherokees

The Cherokees were among the first. They were the first to inhabit the Smokies, the first to leave them and yet remain behind. By the 1600s these Indians had built in the Southern Appalachians a Nation hundreds of years old, a way of life in harmony with the surrounding natural world, a culture richly varied and satisfying. But barely two centuries later, the newly formed government of the United States was pushing the Cherokees ever farther west. In the struggle for homeland, a new era had arrived: a time for the pioneer and for the settler from Europe and the eastern seaboard to stake claims to what seemed to them mere wilderness but which to the Cherokees was a physical and spiritual abode.

Perhaps it was during the last Ice Age that Indians drifted from Asia to this continent across what was then a land passage through Alaska's Bering Strait. Finding and settling various regions of North America, this ancient people fragmented after thousands of years into different tribal and linguistic stocks. The Iroquois, inhabitants of what are now the North Central and Atlantic states, became one of the most distinctive of these stocks.

By the year 1000, the Cherokees, a tribe of Iroquoian origin, had broken off the main line and turned south. Whether wanting to or being pressured to, they slowly followed the mountain leads of the Blue Ridge and the Alleghenies until they reached the security and peace of the mist-shrouded Southern Appalachians. These "Mountaineers," as other Iroquois called them, claimed an empire of roughly 104,000 square kilometers (40,000 square miles). Bounded on the north by the mighty Ohio River, it stretched southward in a great circle through eight states, including half of South Carolina and almost all of Kentucky and Tennessee.

Cherokee settlements dotted much of this territory, particularly in eastern Tennessee, western North Carolina, and northern Georgia. These state regions are the rough outlines of what came to be the three main divisions of the Cherokee Nation: the Lower settlements on the headwaters of the Savannah River in Georgia and South Carolina; the Middle Towns on the Little Tennessee and Tuckasegee rivers in North Carolina; and the Overhill Towns with a capital on the Tellico River in Tennessee.

Between the Middle and the Overhill Cherokee,

The plight of their Cherokee ancestors is revealed in the faces of Kweti and child in this photograph taken by James Mooney.

Adventurers were drawn to the Great Smoky Mountains and the surrounding area in the 18th century. In 1760 a young British agent from Virginia, Lt. Henry Timberlake, journeyed far into Cherokee country. He observed Indian life and even sketched a map of the Overhill territory, complete with Fort Loudoun, "Chote" or Echota, and the "Enemy Mountains."

straddling what is now the North Carolina-Tennessee line, lay the imposing range of the Great Smoky Mountains. Except for Mt. Mitchell in the nearby Blue Ridge, these were the highest mountains east of the Black Hills in South Dakota and the Rockies in Colorado. They formed the heart of the territorial Cherokee Nation. The Oconaluftee River, rushing down to the Tuckasegee from the North Carolina side of the Smokies, watered the homesites and fields of many Cherokees. Kituwah, a Middle Town near the present-day Deep Creek campground, may have been in the first Cherokee village.

For the most part, however, the Cherokees settled only in the foothills of the Smokies. Like the later pioneers, the Cherokees were content with the fertile lands along the rivers and creeks. But more than contentment was involved. Awed by this tangled wilderness, the Indians looked upon these heights as something both sacred and dangerous. One of the strongest of the old Cherokee myths tells of a race of spirits living there in mountain caves. These handsome "Little People" were usually helpful and kind, but they could make the intruder lose his way.

If the Cherokees looked up to the Smokies, they aimed at life around them with a level eye. Although the Spanish explorer Hernando DeSoto and his soldiers ventured through Cherokee country in 1540 and chronicled generally primitive conditions, a Spanish missionary noted 17 years later that the Cherokees appeared "sedate and thoughtful, dwelling in peace in their native mountains; they cultivated their fields and lived in prosperity and plenty."

They were moderately tall and rather slender with long black hair and sometimes very light complexions. They wore animal skin loincloths and robes, moccasins and a knee-length buckskin hunting shirt. A Cherokee man might dress more gaudily than a woman, but both enjoyed decorating their bodies extravagantly, covering themselves with paint and, as trade with whites grew and flourished, jewelry.

The tepee of Indian lore did not exist here. The Cherokee house was a rough log structure with one door and no windows. A small hole in the bark roof allowed smoke from a central fire to escape. Furniture and decorations included cane seats and painted hemp rugs. A good-sized village might number 40 or 50 houses.

Chota, in the Overhill country on the Little Tennessee River, was a center of civil and religious authority; it was also known as a "Town of Refuge," a place of asylum for Indian criminals, especially murderers. The Smokies settlement of Kituwah served as a "Mother Town," or a headquarters, for one of the seven Cherokee clans.

These clans—Wolf, Blue, Paint, Bird, Deer, Long Hair, and Wild Potato—were basic to the social structure of the tribe. The Cherokees traced their kinship by clan; marriage within clans was forbidden. And whereas the broad divisions of Lower, Middle, and Overhill followed natural differences in geography and dialect, the clans assumed great political significance. Each clan selected its own chiefs and its own "Mother Town." Although one or two persons in Chota might be considered symbolic leaders, any chief's powers were limited to advice and persuasion.

The Cherokees extended this democratic tone to all their towns. Each village, whether built along or near a stream or surrounded by protective log palisades, would have as its center a Town House and Square. The Square, a level field in front, was used for celebrations and dancing. The Town House itself sheltered the town council, plus the entire village, during their frequent meetings. In times of decision-making, as many as 500 people crowded into the smoky, earth-domed building where they sat in elevated rows around the council and heard debates on issues from war to the public granary.

Democracy was the keynote of the Cherokee Nation. "White" chiefs served during peacetime; "Red" chiefs served in time of war. Priests once formed a special class, but after an episode in which one of the priests attempted to "take" the wife of the leading chief's brother, all such privileged persons were made to take their place alongside—not in front of—the other members of the community.

Women enjoyed the same status in Cherokee society as men. Clan kinship, land included, followed the mother's side of the family. Although the men hunted much of the time, they helped with some household duties, such as sewing. Marriages were solemnly negotiated. And it was possible for women to sit in the councils as equals to men. Indeed, Nancy Ward, one of those equals who enjoyed the rank of Beloved Woman, did much to strengthen bonds of friendship

between Cherokee and white during the turbulent years of the mid-18th century. The Irishman James Adair, who traded with the Cherokees during the years 1736 to 1743, even accused these Indians of "petticoat government." Yet he must have found certain attractions in this arrangement, for he himself married a Cherokee woman of the Deer Clan.

Adair, an intent observer of Indian life, marveled at the Cherokees' knowledge of nature's medicines: *"I do not remember to have seen or heard of an Indian dying by the bite of a snake, when out at war, or a hunting. . . . they, as well as all other Indian nations, have a great knowledge of specific virtues in simples: applying herbs and plants, on the most dangerous occasions, and seldom if ever, fail to effect a thorough cure, from the natural bush. . . . For my own part, I would prefer an old Indian before any surgeon whatsoever. . . ."*

The Indians marveled at nature itself. A Civil War veteran remarked that the Cherokees "possess a keen and delicate appreciation of the beautiful in nature." Most of their elaborate mythology bore a direct relation to rock and plant, animal and tree, river and sky. One myth told of a tortoise and a hare. The tortoise won the race, but not by steady plodding. He placed his relatives at intervals along the course; the hare, thinking the tortoise was outrunning him at every turn, wore himself out before the finish.

The Cherokees' many myths and their obedience to nature required frequent performance of rituals. There were many nature celebrations, including three each corn season: the first at the planting of this staple crop, the second at the very beginning of the harvest, the third and last and largest at the moment of the fullest ripening. One of the most important rites, the changing of the fire, inaugurated each new year. All flames were extinguished and the hearths were swept clean of ashes. The sacred fire at the center of the Town House was then rekindled.

One ritual aroused particular enthusiasm: war. Battles drew the tribe together, providing an arena for fresh exploits and a common purpose and source of inspiration for the children. The Cherokees, with their spears, bows and arrows, and mallet-shaped clubs, met any challenger: Shawnee, Tuscarora, Creek, English, or American. In 1730, Cherokee chiefs told English emissaries: "Should we make

A Cherokee fishes in the Oconaluftee River.

A team of oxen hauls a sled full of corn stalks for a Cherokee farmer near Ravensford, North Carolina. Oxen were more common beasts of burden in the mountains than horses mainly because they were less expensive.

Pages 40-41: At Ayunini's house a woman pounds corn into meal with a mortar and pestle. The simple, log house is typical of Cherokee homes at the turn of the century. This one has stone chimneys, whereas many merely had a hole in the roof.

peace with the Tuscaroras ... we must immediately look for some other with whom we can be engaged in our beloved occupation." Even in peacetime, the Cherokees might invade settlements just for practice.

But when the white man came, the struggle was for larger stakes. In 1775 William Bartram, the first able native-born American botanist, could explore the dangerous Cherokee country and find artistry there, perfected even in the minor arts of weaving and of carving stone tobacco pipes. He could meet and exchange respects with the famous Cherokee statesman Attakullakulla, also known as the Little Carpenter. And yet, a year later, other white men would destroy more than two-thirds of the settled Cherokee Nation.

Who were these fateful newcomers? Most of them were Scotch-Irish, a distinctive and adventuresome blend of people transplanted chiefly from the Scottish Lowlands to Northern Ireland during the reign of James I. Subsequently they flocked to the American frontier in search of religious freedom, economic opportunity, and new land they could call their own.

In the late 1600s, while the English colonized the Atlantic seaboard in North and South Carolina and Virginia, while the French settled Alabama, Mississippi, and Louisiana ports on the Gulf of Mexico, and while the Spanish pushed into Florida, 5,000 Presbyterian Scots left England for "the Plantation" in Northern Ireland. But as they settled and prospered, England passed laws prohibiting certain articles of Irish trade, excluding Presbyterians from civil and military offices, even declaring their ministers liable to prosecution for performing marriages.

The Scotch-Irish, as they were then called, found such repression unbearable and fled in the early 18th century to ports in Delaware and Pennsylvania. With their influx, Pennsylvania land prices skyrocketed. Poor, rocky soil to the immediate west turned great numbers of these Scotch-Irish southward down Virginia's Shenandoah Valley and along North Carolina's Piedmont plateau. From 1732 to 1754, the population of North Carolina more than doubled. Extravagant stories of this new and fertile land also drew many from the German Palatinate to America; during the middle 1700s these hardworking "Pennsylvania Dutch" poured into the southern colonies.

Virginia, the Carolinas, and Georgia were colonies of the crown, and the Scotch-Irish and Germans intermarried with the already settled British. These Englishmen, of course, had their own reasons for leaving their more conservative countrymen in the mother country and starting a whole new life. Some were adventurers eager to explore a different land, some sought religious freedom, not a few were second sons—victims of the law of primogeniture—who arrived with hopes of building new financial empires of their own. They all confronted the frontier.

They encountered the Cherokee Nation and its vast territory. Earliest relations between the Cherokees and the pioneers were, to say the least, marked by paradox. Traders like James Adair formed economic ties and carried on a heavy commerce of guns for furs, whisky for blankets, jewelry for horses. But there was also deep resentment. The English colonies, especially South Carolina, even took Indian prisoners and sold them into slavery.

The Spanish had practiced this kind of slavery, arguing that thus the Indians would be exposed to the boon of Christianity. The English colonies employed what were known as "indentured servants," persons who paid off the cost of their passage to America by working often as hard as slaves. And in later years both the white man and some of the more prosperous Cherokees kept Negro slaves. Such instances in the Nation were more rare than not, however, and a Cherokee might work side by side with any slave he owned; marriage between them was not infrequent. Be that as it may, the deplorable colonial policy of enforced servitude at any level, which continued into the late 1700s, sowed seeds of bitterness that ended in a bloody harvest.

Like the pioneers, the Cherokees cherished liberty above all else and distrusted government. Both left religion to the family and refused to institute any orthodox system of belief. Even the forms of humor were often parallel; the Cherokee could be as sarcastic as the pioneer and used irony to correct behavior. As one historian put it: "The coward was praised for his valor; the liar for his veracity; and the thief for his honesty." But through the ironies of history, the Scotch-Irish-English-German pioneers of the highlands, who were similar to the Cherokees in a multitude of ways and quite different from the lowland

In 1730, Sir Alexander Cuming took seven Cherokee leaders to England in an attempt to build up good relations with the tribe. Among the group was the youth Ukwaneequa (right), who was to become the great Cherokee chief Attakullakulla.

aristocrats, became the Indians' worst enemy.

Their conflict was, in a sense, inevitable. The countries of England and France and their representatives in America both battled and befriended the Cherokees during the 18th century. Their main concern lay in their own rivalry, not in any deep-founded argument with the Indians. As they expanded the American frontier and immersed themselves in the process of building a country, the colonists inevitably encroached upon the Cherokee Nation.

In 1730, in a burst of freewheeling diplomacy, the British sent a flamboyant and remarkable representative, Sir Alexander Cuming, into remote Cherokee country on a mission of goodwill. After meeting with the Indians on their own terms and terrain, Cuming arranged a massive public relations campaign and escorted Attakullakulla and six other Cherokee leaders to London, where they were showered with gifts and presented at court to King George II. The Cherokees allied themselves with Britain, but this did not discourage the French from trying to win their allegiance. When the English in 1743 captured a persuasive visionary named Christian Priber who sought to transform the Cherokee Nation into a socialist utopia, they suspected him of being a French agent and took him to prison in Frederica, Georgia. He was left to die in the fort.

The British soldiers were not as friendly as British diplomats. During the French and Indian War of the late 1750s and the early 1760s, when England battled France for supremacy in the New World, English soldiers treated the Cherokees with disdain and violence. The Cherokees returned the atrocities in kind. The frontier blazed with death and destruction; each side accumulated its own collection of horrors endured and meted out. Although Cherokee chiefs sued for peace, Gov. William Henry Lyttleton of South Carolina declared war on them in 1759. The Carolinas offered 25 English pounds for every Indian scalp. A year later the Cherokees, under the command of Oconostota, captured Fort Loudoun at the fork of the Tellico and Little Tennessee rivers. But in June of 1761, Capt. James Grant and some 2,600 men destroyed the Nation's Middle Towns, burning 600 hectares (1,500 acres) of corn, beans, and peas, and forcing 5,000 Cherokees into the forests for the winter.

After the English defeated the French in 1763, the British government moved to appease the Indians and consolidate its control of the continent. A British proclamation forbade all white settlement beyond the Appalachian divide. But the proclamation was soon to be broken. Pioneers such as Daniel Boone and James Robertson successfully led their own and neighbors' families through Appalachian gaps and river valleys until a trickle of explorers became a flood of homesteaders. During the next decade, settlers poured across the mountains into Kentucky and northeastern Tennessee.

While England was regaining the friendship of the Cherokees, the American colonists were alienating both the Indians and the British. In the late 1760s a group of North Carolinians calling themselves Regulators opposed taxation, land rents, and extensive land grants to selected individuals, and caused unrest throughout the Piedmont. In 1771, at Alamance, an estimated 2,000 Regulators were defeated by the troops of British Gov. William Tryon. Thousands of anti-royalist North Carolinians fled westward as a result of this battle. Alexander Cameron, an English representative living in the Overhill Towns, wrote in 1766 that the pioneer occupation of Cherokee lands amounted to an infestation by villains and horse thieves that was "enough to create disturbances among the most Civilized Nations."

The protest spirit of the Regulators spread to the New England colonies during the early 1770s. By 1776, when the American Revolution began, the Cherokees had understandably but unfortunately chosen to take the British side. Britain issued guns to all Indians and offered rewards for American scalps, yet this was not enough to secure the over-mountain territory for the English crown. Within a year, American forces were fighting for the frontier, and in a coordinated pincer movement, Col. Samuel Jack with 200 Georgians, Gen. Griffith Rutherford with 2,400 North Carolinians, Col. Andrew Williamson with 1,800 South Carolinians, and Col. William Christian with 2,000 Virginians demolished more than 50 Cherokee towns. Two treaties resulted from this campaign; more than 2 million hectares (5 million acres) of Indian land, including northeastern Tennessee, much of South Carolina, and all lands east of the Blue Ridge, were ceded to the United States.

Peace did not follow the treaties, however. Dragging Canoe, pock-marked son of Attakullakulla, decided to fight. Against the wishes of many Cherokee chiefs, he organized a renegade tribe that moved to five Lower Towns near present-day Chattanooga where they became known as the Chickamaugas. But the eventual outcome of the drama had already been determined. Despite conflict and danger, the settlers pushed on. In 1780 the Tennesseans John Sevier and Isaac Shelby joined forces with those of William Campbell from Virginia and Joseph McDowell from North Carolina and managed to win a decisive victory over the English at Kings Mountain, South Carolina. By fighting Indian-style on rugged hillside terrain, they overwhelmed a detachment of General Cornwallis' southern forces under Col. Patrick Ferguson. These over-mountain men immediately returned to Tennessee and in reprisal for Indian raids during their absence destroyed Chota and nine other Overhill Towns, slaughtering women and children as well as Cherokee warriors.

In 1783, with the end of the Revolution, all hope for the survival of the original Cherokee Nation was extinguished. Although the newly formed American government attempted to conciliate the Indians, it could not prevent its own citizens from hungering for ever larger bites of land. Treaties with the loose Cherokee confederation of clans became more and more frequent. As if by fate, a disastrous smallpox epidemic struck the Cherokees; the number of warriors dwindled to less than half of what it had been 50 years before. The Cherokee capital was moved from Chota southward into Georgia. In 1794 Maj. James Ore and 550 militiamen from Nashville, Tennessee, obliterated the Chickamaugas and their Five Towns.

Most of the Cherokees parted with the Smokies. At the Treaty of Holston in 1791, they gave up the northeastern quarter of what is now the park. Seven years later, they ceded a southern strip. And at Washington, D.C., in February of 1819, nearly a century after their first treaty with the white man in 1721, the Cherokees signed their 21st treaty. This time they parted with a quarter of their entire Nation, and they lost the rest of their sacred Smoky Mountains. Scattered families continued to live in the foothills. But the newcomer—this pioneer turned settler—had arrived.

Ayunini, or Swimmer, was a medicine man. He was a major source of information about Cherokee history, mythology, botany, and medicine when James Mooney of the Bureau of American Ethnology visited the area in 1888.

The Pioneers Arrive

Into the Smokies they came, but the coming was slow. The early pioneers of the Old Southwest had conquered the lowlands of North Carolina and Tennessee with relative ease. The higher country of the Great Smoky Mountains, set into the Southern Appalachians like a great boulder among scattered stones, would yield less quickly.

The pioneers began, as the Cherokees had done, with the most accessible land. The level Oconaluftee valley, stretching its timbered swath from present-day Cherokee, North Carolina, on up into the forks and tributaries of the Great Smokies, beckoned with at least some possibilities to the hopeful settler. As early as 1790, Dr. Joseph Dobson, a North Carolina Revolutionary War veteran who had accompanied Rutherford on his 1777 campaign against the Cherokees, entered into deed a tract on the Oconaluftee. But the claim was void; the valley still belonged to the Indians.

John Walker had also ridden with Rutherford. His son Felix, a student and friend of Dr. Dobson, lawfully received in 1795 a sizable land grant to the valley. Young Walker was more than willing to let settlers attempt development of this wild area. Two North Carolina families decided to try. John Jacob Mingus and Ralph Hughes took their wives and children and journeyed into the "Lufty" regions of the Smokies. They cleared small homesteads by the river; they were all alone.

In 1803, Abraham Enloe and his family moved up from South Carolina and joined the growing families of Mingus and Hughes. Enloe chose land directly across the river from John Mingus, and by 1820 Abraham's daughter Polly had married John, junior. "Dr. John," as the younger Mingus was respectfully called in his later years, learned much about medicine from the scattered Cherokees remaining in the area.

Other families, Carolinian and Georgian and Virginian alike, arrived and stayed. Collins, Bradley, Beck, Conner, Floyd, Sherrill: these and others settled beside the river itself, and their children moved along the creeks and branches. Fresh lands were cleared, new homes built; the Oconaluftee was being transformed. And further to the southwest, Forney Creek was being claimed by Crisps and Monteiths, Coles and Welches; Deep Creek had already been

Between her many had-to-be-done tasks around the house, Mollie McCarter Ogle rocks her daughter Mattie on the porch.

colonized by Abraham Wiggins and his descendants.

The Tennessee side of the Smokies, furrowed by its own series of rivers and creeks, awaited settlement. By 1800 a few Virginians and Carolinians were drifting into the four-year-old state of Tennessee, willing to settle.

The first family of Gatlinburg was probably a mother and her seven children. This widow, Martha Huskey Ogle, brought five sons and two daughters from Edgefield, South Carolina. Richard Reagan, a Scotch-Irishman from Virginia, and his family joined the Ogles and began to clear land. His son, Daniel Wesley Reagan, born in 1802, was the first child of the settlement and later became a leading citizen of the community. The elder Reagan was fatally injured when a heavy wind blew the limb from a tree on him, reminding the little community once more of the precarious nature of survival in this free, stern country.

Maples, Clabos, and Trenthams followed the Ogles and the Reagans into the Gatlinburg area. Nearby Big Greenbrier Cove became known as "the Whaley Settlement." Some settlers traveled directly across the crest of the Smokies, via Indian and Newfound Gaps, but these old Cherokee trails and cattle paths were rough and overgrown. Horses could barely make it through, and most possessions had to be carried on stout human shoulders. Besides the usual pots, tools, guns, and seeds were the Bibles and treasured manmade mementos.

Many settlers, having been soldiers of the Revolution, had received 20-hectare (50-acre) land grants for a mere 75 cents. They pushed along the West Prong of the Little Pigeon River, past Gatlinburg, up among the steep slopes of the Bull Head, the Chimney Tops, the Sugarland Mountain. This narrow Sugarlands valley, strewn with water-smoothed boulders and homestead-sized plateaus of level land, attracted dozens of families. But this rocky country forced the settlers to clear their fields twice, first of the forest and then of the stones.

The work of clearing demanded strong muscles, long hours, and sturdy spirits. It meant denting the hard armor of the forest and literally fighting for a tiny patch of cropland. Men axed the huge trees with stroke after grinding stroke, then either wrenched the stumps from the earth with teams of oxen or burned them when they had dried. Some trees were so immense that all a man could do was "girdle" them, which meant deep-cutting a fatal circle into the bark to arrest the flow of sap. Such "deadenings" might stand for years with crops planted on the "new ground," before the trees were finally cut and often burned. Logs and stumps from the virgin forest often smouldered for days or weeks.

The soil itself was rich and loamy with the topsoil of centuries. Land that had produced great forests could also nourish fine crops. During the first year of settlement, all able-bodied members of the family helped cultivate the new ground. Such land demanded particular attention. Using a single-pointed "Bull tongue" plow to bite deep into the earth and a sharp iron "coulter" to cut tough roots left under the massive stumps, a succession of plows, horses, and workers prepared and turned the newly cleared field. The first man "laid off" the rows into evenly spaced lengths, the second plowed an adjacent furrow, and the wife or children dropped in the seed. A third plow covered this planted row by furrowing along its side. A short while later, the same workers would "bust middles" by plowing three extra furrows into the ground between the seeded rows. This loosened the soil and destroyed any remaining roots.

Uncle George Lamon sits next to one of his honey bee boxes at his home in Gumstand, near Gatlinburg.

While fields throughout the Smokies were yielding to the plow, even more isolated coves and creeks were being penetrated and settled. Gunters, Webbs, McGahas, and Suttons found their way into Big Creek. And in 1818, John Oliver walked into a secluded Tennessee cove, spent the night in an Indian hut, and then became familiar with one of the most beautiful and productive spots in all the Great Smokies. This broad, well-watered basin of fertile land was named after the wife of an old Cherokee chief; it was called Kate's Cove, later Cades Cove.

John Oliver settled in that cove. Three years later— two years after the decisive 1819 treaty with the Cherokees—William Tipton settled there legally, bought up most of the land, and parceled it out to paying newcomers. David Foute came and established an iron forge in 1827. By mixing iron ore with limestone and charcoal, this "bloomery forge" produced chunks of iron called "blooms." The forge, similar to many which sprang up throughout Appalachia, was indeed an asset, but its low-grade

Most families had several scaffolds in their yards on which they dried fruits, beans, corn, and even duck and chicken feathers for stuffing pillows.

Near most houses was a smokehouse in which meat was cured and often stored for later use.

Fruits and other goods were stored in barns or sheds, often located over cool springs.

ore and the cost of charcoal forced it to close only 20 years later.

Russell Gregory built a homestead high in the cove and ranged cattle on a nearby grassy bald. These mysterious open meadows scattered throughout the Smokies were of unknown origin. Had Indians kept them cleared in years gone by? Had some unexplained natural circumstance created them? Pioneers and later experts alike remained baffled and attracted by the lush grass which, growing among forest-covered crags and pinnacles, provided excellent forage for livestock. The present-day Parson's and Gregory Balds were named for enterprising farmers who made early use of this phenomenon. Peter Cable, a friend of William Tipton, joined the valley settlement in Cades Cove. Cable's son-in-law, Dan Lawson, expanded Cable's holdings into a narrow mountain-to-mountain empire.

Cades Cove, with its vast farmland, soon rivaled Oconaluftee and Cataloochee. The lower end of the cove sometimes became swampy, but this pasture was reclaimed by a series of dikes and log booms. To escape an 1825 epidemic of typhoid in the Tennessee lowlands, Robert Shields and his family moved up into the hill-guarded cove. Two of his sons married John Oliver's daughters and remained in Cades Cove. A community had been formed.

But the life in these small communities was not easy. Each family farmed for a living; each family homestead provided for its own needs and such luxuries as it could create. Isolation from outside markets made cash crops, and hence cash itself, relatively insignificant. The settlers of the Great Smokies depended upon themselves. They built their own cabins and corncribs, their own meat- and apple- and spring-houses. They cultivated a garden whose corn, potatoes, and other vegetables would last the family through the winter. They set about insuring a continuous supply of pork and fruit and grains, wool and sometimes cotton, and all the other commodities necessary to keep a family alive.

Living off the land required both labor and ingenuity. These early settlers did not mind fishing and hunting for food throughout the spring, summer, and early fall, but there were also the demands of farming and livestock raising. They carved out of wood such essentials as ox yokes and wheat cradles,

Alden Stevens

spinning wheels and looms. Men patiently rebuilt and repaired anything from a broken harness to a sagging "shake" roof made of hand-riven shingles. Children picked quantities of wild berries and bushels of beans in sun-hot fields and gathered eggs from hidden hen nests in barn lofts and under bushes. They found firewood for the family, carried water from the spring, bundled fodder from cane and corn, and stacked hay for the cattle, horses, mules, and oxen.

Women made sure that the food supply stretched to last through the winter. They helped salt and cure pork from the hogs that their husbands slaughtered. They employed a variety of methods to preserve vital fruits and vegetables. Apples, as well as beans, were carefully dried in the hot summer or autumn sun; water, added months later, would restore a tangy flavor. Some foods were pickled in brine or vinegar.

Women also used sulphur as a preservative, especially with apples. Called simply "fruit" by the early settlers, apples such as the favorite Limbertwigs and Milams gave both variety and nutrition to the pioneer diet. A woman might peel and slice as much as two dishpans of "fruit" into a huge barrel. She would then lay a pan of sulphur on top of the apples and light the contents. By covering the barrel with a clean cloth, she could regulate the right amount of fumes held inside. The quickly sulfurated apples remained white all winter and were considered a delicacy by every mountain family.

Food, clothing, shelter, and incessant labor: these essentials formed only the foundation of a life. Intangible forces hovered at the edges and demanded fulfillment. As hardy and practical as the physical existence of the pioneers had to be, there was another dimension to life. The pioneers were human beings. Often isolated, sometimes lonely, they yearned for the comforts of myth and superstition and religion—and the roads that led in and out. The Cherokees in their time had created such comforts; they had woven their myths and had laced the Smokies with a network of trails. Now it was the white man's turn.

The early settlers of the Great Smoky Mountains were not content to remain only in their hidden hollows and on their tiny homesteads. Challenging

In the days before refrigerators, many methods and kinds of containers were used in preserving and storing foods. Corn meal, dried beans and other vegetables, and sulphured fruits were kept in bins made from hollow black gum logs.

Food also was stored in pie safes. The pierced tin panels allow air into the cabinet but prevent flies from getting at the food.

Edouard E. Exline

the mountain ranges and the rough terrain, they constructed roads. In the mid-1830s, a project was undertaken to lay out a road across the crest of the Smokies and connect North Carolina's Little Tennessee valley with potential markets in Knoxville, Tennessee. Although the North Carolina section was never completed, an old roadbed from Cades Cove to Spence Field is still in existence. When Julius Gregg established a licensed distillery in Cades Cove and processed brandy from apples and corn, farmers built a road from the cove down Tabcat Creek to the vast farmlands along the Little Tennessee River.

By far the most ambitious road project was the Oconaluftee Turnpike. In 1832, the North Carolina legislature chartered the Oconaluftee Turnpike Company. Abraham Enloe, Samuel Sherrill, John Beck, John Carroll, and Samuel Gibson were commissioners for the road and were authorized to sell stock and collect tolls. The road itself was to run from Oconaluftee all the way to the top of the Smokies at Indian Gap.

Work on the road progressed slowly. Bluffs and cliffs had to be avoided; such detours lengthened the turnpike considerably. Sometimes the rock was difficult to remove. Crude blasting—complete with hand-hammered holes, gunpowder inside hollow reeds, and fuses of straw or leaves—constituted one quick and sure, but more expensive, method. Occasionally, the men burned logs around the rock, then quickly showered it with creek water. When the rock split from the sudden change in temperature, it could then be quarried and graded out. Throughout the 1830s, residents of Oconaluftee and nearby valleys toiled and sweated to lay down this single roadbed.

This desire and effort to conquer the wilderness also prompted the establishment of churches and, to a lesser extent, schools. In the Tennessee Sugarlands, services were held under the trees until a small building was constructed at the beginning of the 19th century. The valley built a larger five-cornered Baptist church in 1816. Prospering Cades Cove established a Methodist church in 1830; its preacher rode the Little River circuit. Five years later, the church had 40 members.

Over on the Oconaluftee, Ralph Hughes had donated land and Dr. John Mingus had built a log schoolhouse. Monthly prayer meetings were held there until the Lufty Baptist Church was officially organized in 1836. Its 21 charter members included most of the turnpike commissioners plus the large Mingus family. Five years later, the members built a log church at Smokemont on land donated by John Beck.

Nothing fostered these settlers' early gropings toward community more than stories. Legends and tall tales, begun in family conversations and embellished by neighborly rumor, forged a bond, a unity of interest, a common history, in each valley and on each meandering branch. For example, in one western North Carolina tradition that would thrive well into the 20th century, Abraham Enloe was cited as the real father of Abraham Lincoln. Nancy Hanks, it was asserted, had worked for a time in the Enloe household and had become pregnant. Exiled to Kentucky, she married Thomas Lincoln but gave birth to Abraham's child.

Stories mingled with superstition. The Cherokees dropped seven grains into every corn hill and never thinned their crop. Many early settlers of the Smokies believed that if corn came up missing in spots, some of the family would die within a year. Just as the Cherokees forbade counting green melons or stepping across the vines because "it would make the vines wither," the Smokies settlers looked upon certain events as bad omens. A few days before Richard Reagan's skull was fractured, a bird flew on the porch where he sat and came to rest on his head. Reagan himself saw it as a "death sign."

Superstition, combined with Indian tradition, led to a strangely exact form of medicine. One recipe for general aches and pains consisted of star root, sourwood, rosemary, sawdust, anvil dust, water, and vinegar. A bad memory required a properly "sticky" tea made of cocklebur and jimsonweed.

A chief medicinal herb was an unusual wild plant known as ginseng. Called "sang" in mountain vernacular, its value lay in the manlike shape of its dual-pronged roots. Oriental cultures treasured ginseng, especially the older and larger roots. Reputed to cure anything from a cough to a boil to an internal disorder, it was also considered an aphrodisiac and a source of rare, mystical properties. But scientific research has never yielded any hard evidence of its medicinal worth.

Aunt Sophie Campbell made clay pipes at her place on Crockett Mountain and sold them to her neighbors and to other folks in the Gatlinburg area.

Alan Rinehart

Settlers used ginseng sparingly, for it brought a high price when sold to herb-dealers for shipment to China. The main problem lay in locating the five-leaved plants, which grew in the most secluded, damp coves of the Smokies. Sometimes several members of a family would wait until summer or early fall, then go out on extended "sanging" expeditions.

The search was not easy. During some seasons, the plant might not appear at all. When it did, its leaves yellowed and its berries reddened for only a few days. But when a healthy "sang" plant was finally found, and its long root carefully cleaned and dried, it could yield great financial reward. Although the 5-year-old white root was more common, a red-rooted plant needed a full decade to mature and was therefore especially prized. Greed often led to wanton destruction of the beds, with no seed-plants for future harvests. Ginseng was almost impossible to cultivate.

Ginseng-hunting became a dangerous business. Although Daniel Boone dug it and traded in it, later gatherers were sometimes killed over it. One large Philadelphia dealer who came into Cataloochee in the mid-1800s was murdered and robbed. Anyone trying to grow it, even if he were successful, found that he would have to guard the plants like water in a desert. Indeed, the rare, graceful ginseng became a symbol for many in the mountains of all that was unique, so readily destroyed, and eventually irreplaceable.

As much as the pioneers drew on Indian experience, they also depended on their own resourcefulness. One skill which the early settlers brought with them into the Smoky Mountains involved a power unknown to the Cherokees. This was the power of the rifle: both its manufacture and the knowledge of what the rifle could do.

The backwoods rifle was a product of the early American frontier. Formally known as the "Pennsylvania-Kentucky" rifle, this long-barreled innovation became a standby throughout the Applachians. To assure precise workmanship, it was made out of the softest iron available. The inside of the barrel, or the bore, was painstakingly "rifled" with spiralling grooves. This gradual twist made the bullet fly harder and aim straighter toward its target. The butt of the weapon was crescent-shaped to keep the gun from slipping. All shiny or highly visible metal was blackened, and sometimes a frontiersman would rub his gun barrel with a dulling stain or crushed leaf.

But the trademark of the "long rifle" was just that: its length. Weighing over 2.5 kilograms (5.5 pounds) and measuring more than 1.2 meters (4 feet), the barrel of the backwoods rifle could be unbalancing. Yet this drawback seemed minor compared to the superior accuracy of the new gun. The heavy barrel could take a much heavier powder charge than the lighter barrels, and this in turn could, as an expert noted, "drive the bullet faster, lower the trajectory, make the ball strike harder, and cause it to flatten out more on impact. It does not cause inaccurate flight...."

The Pennsylvania-Kentucky rifle became defender, gatherer of food, companion for thousands of husbands and fathers. Cradled on a rack of whittled wooden pegs or a buck's antlers, the "rifle-gun" hung over the door or along the wall or above the "fire-board," as the mantel was called, within easy and ready reach. It was the recognized symbol of the fact that each man's cabin was his castle.

Equipped with a weapon such as this, pioneer Americans pushed back the frontier. The fastnesses of the Great Smoky Mountains gradually submitted to the probing and settling of the white man. The fertile valleys were settled, the hidden coves were conquered. The Oconaluftee Turnpike to the top of the Smokies was completed in 1839. And in that fateful year, disaster was stalking a people who had known the high mountains but who had not known of the ways of making a rifle.

A young Smokies lad stands proudly with his long rifle and powder horn before heading off to the woods on a hunting excursion.

Rifle Making

Of all the special tasks in the Great Smoky Mountains, rifle making was perhaps the most intricate and the most intriguing. From the forging of the barrel to the filing of the double trigger and the carving of the stock, the construction of the "long rifle" proved to be a process both painstaking and exciting. After the barrel was shaped on the anvil, its bore was cleaned to a glass-like finish by inserting and turning an iron rod with steel cutters. When the rod could cut no more, the shavings from the bore were

National Park Service

removed. The rifling of the barrel, or cutting the necessary twists into the bore, required a 3-meters-long (10-foot) assembly, complete with barrel, cutting rod, and rifling guide. The 1.5-meter (5-foot) wooden guide, whose parallel twists had been carefully cut into it with a knife, could be turned by a man pushing it through the spiral-edged hole of a stationary "head block." The resulting force and spin drove the cutting rod and its tiny saw into the barrel, guiding its movement as it "rifled" the gun.

Charles S. Grossman

Most of the rifles in the Smokies had an average spin or twist of about one turn in 122 centimeters (48 inches), the ordinary original length of the barrel. A later step—"dressing out" the barrel with a greased hickory stick and a finishing saw—usually took a day and a half to be done right. Likewise, the making of a maple or walnut rifle stock, or the forging of the bullet mold, led gunsmiths to adopt the long view of time and the passing of days in the Great Smoky Mountains. Two such gunsmiths were Matt Ownby and Wiley Gibson. Ownby (far left) fits a barrel to an unfinished stock as the process of rifle making nears its end. Gibson (below), the last of four generations of famous Smoky Mountain gunsmiths, works at his forge in Sevier County, Tennessee. Over the years Gibson lived in several places in Sevier County, and in each one he set up a gun shop. As he tested one of his finished products (left), Gibson commented: "I can knock a squirrel pine blank out of a tree at 60 yards."

A Band of Cherokees Holds On

The Cherokees who remained in the East endured many changes in the early 1800s.

As their Nation dwindled in size to cover only portions of Georgia, Alabama, North Carolina, and Tennessee, the influence of growing white settlements began to encroach on the old ways, the accepted beliefs. Settlers intermarried with Indians. Aspects of the Nation's civilization gradually grew to resemble that of the surrounding states.

The Cherokees diversified and improved their agricultural economy. They came to rely more heavily on livestock. Herds of sheep, goats, and hogs, as well as cattle, grazed throughout the Nation. Along with crops of aromatic tobacco, and such staples as squash, potatoes, beans, and the ever-present corn, the Cherokees were cultivating cotton, grains, indigo, and other trade items. Boats carried tons of export to New Orleans and other river cities. Home industry, such as spinning and weaving, multiplied; local merchants thrived.

Church missions and their attendant schools were established. As early as 1801, members of the Society of United Brethren set up a station of missionaries at a north Georgia site called Spring Place. And within five years, the Rev. Gideon Blackburn from East Tennessee persuaded his Presbyterians to subsidize two schools.

In 1817, perhaps the most famous of all the Cherokee missions was opened on Chickamauga Creek at Brainerd, just across the Tennessee line from Georgia. Founded by Cyrus Kingsbury and a combined Congregational-Presbyterian board, Brainerd Mission educated many Cherokee leaders, including Elias Boudinot and John Ridge. Samuel Austin Worcester, a prominent Congregational minister from New England, taught at Brainerd from 1825 until 1834. He became a great friend of the Cherokees and was referred to as "The Messenger."

In 1821, a single individual gave to his Nation an educational innovation as significant and far-reaching as the influx of schools. A Cherokee named Sequoyah, known among whites as George Gist, had long been interested in the "talking leaves" of the white man. After years of thought, study, and hard work, he devised an 86-character Cherokee alphabet. Born about 1760 near old Fort Loudoun, Tennessee, Sequoyah had neither attended school nor learned

Walini was among the Cherokees living on the Qualla Reservation in North Carolina when James Mooney visited in 1888.

Sequoyah displays the Cherokee alphabet he developed.

English. By 1818, he had moved to Willstown in what is now eastern Alabama and had grown interested in the white man's ability to write. He determined that he would give his own people the same advantage.

The first painstaking process he tried called for attaching a mark to each Cherokee word. These marks soon mounted into the thousands. As he sensed the futility of this one-for-one relationship, he examined English letters in an old newspaper. His own mind linked symbols of this sort with basic sounds of the Cherokee tongue. After months of work, he sorted out these sounds and assigned them symbols based, to a large extent, upon the ones he had seen in the newspaper. When he introduced his invention to his fellow Cherokees, it was as if he had loosed a floodgate. Within the space of a few weeks, elders and children alike began to read and write. The change was incredible.

Sequoyah himself vaulted into a position of great respect inside the Nation. One of his many awestruck visitors, John Howard Payne, described him with the finest detail and noted that Sequoyah wore
". . . a turban of roses and posies upon a white ground girding his venerable grey hairs, a long dark blue robe, bordered around the lower edge and the cuffs, with black; a blue and white minutely checked calico tunic under it, confined with an Indian beaded belt, which sustained a large wooden handled knife, in a rough leather sheath; the tunic open on the breast and its collar apart, with a twisted handkerchief flung around his neck and gathered within the bosom of the tunic. He wore plain buckskin leggings; and one of a deeper chocolate hue than the other. His moccasins were unornamented buckskin. He had a long dusky white bag of sumac with him, and a long Indian pipe, and smoked incessantly, replenishing his pipe from his bag. His air was altogether what we picture to ourselves of an old Greek philosopher. He talked and gesticulated very gracefully; his voice alternately swelling, and then sinking to a whisper, and his eye firing up and then its wild flashes subsiding into a gentle and most benignant smile."
During the 1820s, Sequoyah moved west to Arkansas. Preoccupied with the legend of a lost band of Cherokees somewhere in the Rocky Mountains, he initiated several attempts to discover the group. But age caught up with him. He died

alone in northern Mexico in the summer of 1843. He had brought his Nation a long way. His name would be immortalized in the great redwood tree of the Far West, the giant sequoia. And in a sense his spirit lived on in the first Cherokee newspaper—the *Cherokee Phoenix*—which was established in 1828 at New Echota, with Elias Boudinot as its editor and Samuel Worcester as its business manager.

The Cherokees also made remarkable changes in government. In 1808, they adopted a written legal code; a dozen years later, they divided the Nation into judicial districts and designated judges. The first Supreme Court of the Cherokees was established in 1822, and by 1827 the Nation had drawn up an American-based Constitution. The president of the constitutional convention was a 37-year-old leader named John Ross. A year later, he began a 40-year term as principal chief of his people.

But whatever the progress of the internal affairs of the Cherokee Nation, political relations with the United States steadily disintegrated. Although the first quarter of the 19th century saw a sympathetic man, Return Jonathan Meigs, serve as America's southern Indian agent, even he and his position could not prevent the relentless pursuit of Indian territory.

In 1802 and 1803, the U.S. Government set a dangerous precedent for the Cherokees. In return for Georgia's abandonment of her claims to the Mississippi Territory, the United States agreed to extinguish all Indian titles for lands lying within Georgia. This indicated that the government was no longer prepared to defend the Cherokee Nation.

President Thomas Jefferson acted to alleviate some of the Cherokee loss. He suggested a program of removal west to a portion of the newly acquired Louisiana Purchase. Most Cherokees hated the plan, yet some harassed bands made the trip to what is now Arkansas. The foot was in the door; hereafter, the government could point to a few Cherokees in Arkansas and direct others there. Even though 800 eastern Cherokee warriors fought alongside Americans during the War of 1812, the United States came to recognize only the government of the Cherokees West.

But what of the Cherokees East? They waited. They pursued daily routines while the pressures around them gathered and grew. And by 1828, these

Students stand before the original school building at Dwight Mission, the first Cherokee mission west of the Mississippi River. The one-room log schoolhouse is very much like those the white settlers built and used for years in the Smokies.

John Ross remained firm in his opposition to the removal of the Cherokees. He was in the last group to leave.

Elias Boudinot (top), editor of the Cherokee Phoenix, *bowed to pressure and joined those willing to move west.*

pressures had reached a degree which showed the Cherokees that the final crush was on.

It began inside the Nation. In the winter of 1828, an old Cherokee councilman, Whitepath, rose up in rebellion against the new constitution. Suspicious of the Nation's whirlwind progress, fearful of the Nation's stormy enemies, Whitepath attempted to persuade his 15,000 countrymen to hold fast to the ways of the past. He assembled a series of localized meetings, where he advocated the abandonment of white religion, society, economy. He called for a return to tribal organization, but his call fell on younger ears and his plan was doomed to failure.

The Cherokees turned to John Ross for leadership. Like Sequoyah, John Ross possessed both grace and ability. These assets, combined with courage, enabled him to accomplish seemingly remote goals for his people. This handsome statesman, educated by his own father, represented the middle ground of Cherokee policy. Though refusing the reactionism of a Whitepath, John Ross also rejected any proposal to move west. For he knew that his people had lived here in the Smokies and belonged here, and he would not have them forced from their homeland.

Andrew Jackson would. This stern Tennessee soldier and politician began his career as a headlong Indian fighter and never lost the zeal. Although Jackson the soldier had been aided numerous times by Cherokee warriors, Jackson the politician was determined to move the Cherokees west. And in the watershed years of 1828 and 1829, Andrew Jackson was elected and sworn in as President of the United States.

Events conspired against the Nation. In July of 1829, in what is now known as Lumpkin County, Georgia, a few shiny nuggets of gold were discovered on Ward's Creek of the Chestatee River. Within days, fortune hunters swarmed into the territory; more than 10,000 gold-seekers squatted on Cherokee lands, disregarded Cherokee rights, and pillaged Cherokee homes. With Jackson's support, the Georgia legislature passed laws confiscating Indian land, nullifying Indian law, and prohibiting Indian assembly. By the end of 1829, the script for Cherokee removal had been blazoned in gold.

But there was more. Andrew Jackson asked Congress for "a general removal law" that would give him prime authority in the matter at the same time that it formed the basis for future treaty negotiation. Congress passed the Removal Act, which included a half-million dollar appropriation for that purpose, in May of 1830. Davy Crockett, whose legendary exploits and down-to-earth compassion made him perhaps the best representative of the mountain spirit, was a U.S. congressman at the time. Although his grandfather had been murdered by Dragging Canoe, Davy Crockett argued against and voted against the bill. He was the only Tennessean to do so, and he was defeated when he ran for reelection.

Cherokee leaders sought help from the U.S. courts. Their friend and missionary, sober and troubled Samuel Worcester, fell victim to a Georgia law "prohibiting the unauthorized residence of white men within the Cherokee Nation." Worcester appealed to the Supreme Court, which in February of 1832 considered the case of *Worcester v. Georgia*. On March 3, a feeble Chief Justice John Marshall read the Court's decision to a packed room: all the Georgia laws against the Cherokee Nation were declared unconstitutional.

Elias Boudinot, editor of the *Phoenix* and a special friend of Worcester, wrote to his brother and expressed the Nation's joy and relief:

"It is glorious news. The laws of the state are declared by the highest judicial tribunal in the country to be null and void. *It is a great triumph on the part of the Cherokees. . . . The question is forever settled as to who is right and who is wrong."*

Yet Andrew Jackson would not stand for such a settlement. "John Marshall has made his decision," Jackson thundered, "now let him enforce it." This was the single instance in American history where the President so bluntly and openly defied a Supreme Court ruling. The situation grew more bleak. Worcester was released from jail only after appealing to the "good will" of the state of Georgia. Matters worsened as Georgia conducted its Cherokee Lottery of 1832, and thousands of white men descended onto lots carved out of the Cherokee land.

Boudinot and several other Cherokee leaders, including John Ridge, grew discouraged to the point of resignation. Jackson's attitude as President, coupled with Georgia's unrelenting attack and the Supreme

Major Ridge signed a treaty ceding all of the Cherokees' land in the east to the United States. He, his son John, and his nephew Elias Boudinot were "executed" on June 22, 1839.

Court's inability to stop it, caused a change of heart in Boudinot and Ridge. Boudinot stepped down from the *Phoenix* and, with Major Ridge, became an important spokesman for a minority faction of Cherokees which was prepared to move west. However, John Ross continued to speak for the vast majority who rejected any discussion of removal.

By 1835, the rift between the Ridge party and John Ross' followers had become open and intense. Seeking to take advantage of this division, Jackson appointed a New York minister, J.F. Schermerhorn, to deal with Boudinot and Ridge. The Cherokee supporters of Ross hated this "loose Dutch Presbyterian minister" and referred to him as "The Devil's Horn."

On several occasions, Ross attempted to negotiate a reasonable solution with Washington. He was frustrated at every turn. In November of 1835, he and the visiting John Howard Payne were arrested by the Georgia militia. In jail, Payne heard a Georgia guard singing "Home Sweet Home" outside his cell. Payne asked the man if he knew that his prisoner had written the song; the guard seemed unimpressed. After spending nine days in jail, Ross and Payne were released without any explanation for their treatment.

Ross traveled on to Washington to resume negotiations. While he was there, Schermerhorn and the Ridge party drew up and signed a treaty. Endorsed by a scant one-tenth of the Nation's 16,000 Cherokees, this treaty ceded to the United States all eastern territory in exchange for $5 million and a comparable amount of western land. Cherokees throughout the Nation registered shock and betrayal; Boudinot and Ridge, their lives already threatened numerous times, would be murdered within four years. Yet despite Ross' protestations of fraud, the U.S. Senate ratified the minority Treaty of New Echota by one vote. A new President, Martin Van Buren, authorized Gen. Winfield Scott to begin the removal of all Cherokees in the summer of 1838.

Scott, while determined to carry out the removal, tried in vain to restrain his troops from inflicting undue hardships. Scott's soldiers moved relentlessly through the Nation. As one private remembered it in later years:

"Men working in the fields were arrested and driven to the stockades. Women were dragged from their

homes by soldiers whose language they could not understand. Children were often separated from their parents and driven into the stockades with the sky for a blanket and earth for a pillow."

The soldiers built 13 stockades in North Carolina, Georgia, Tennessee, and Alabama. Using these as base camps, they scattered throughout the countryside with loaded rifles and fixed bayonets. As they herded Indians back toward the forts, bands of roving outlaws burned the homes, stole the livestock, robbed the graves. Throughout the summer, a stifling drought settled over the hot, depleted Nation. By August, many of the captured Cherokees had succumbed to sickness or even death.

Removal itself began during the autumn. A few early contingents had been moved out along the Tennessee River in large two-decker keelboats. The majority would travel overland. Thirteen detachments of about 1,000 each, plus 645 wagons carrying the sick and aged, departed from southeastern Tennessee. Early on in their journey, the weather changed. Winter stalked the doomed procession with the tenacity of a bloodhound. By the time the Cherokees crossed the Mississippi River many had died because of lack of food and warmth. In March of 1839, the dwindling band reached what is now Oklahoma. Four thousand Cherokees, almost one-third of all who left their mountain homeland, had been taken by the cold, hard hand of death.

The tragedy would be recorded in history as the "Trail of Tears." Along the route, old Whitepath died. The wife of John Ross gave her blanket to a sick child and herself suffered fatal exposure. A white Georgia volunteer summarized the needless pain in one short sentence: "That Cherokee removal was the cruelest work I ever knew." But disaster was not the final conqueror. For out of that cruelty came sacrifice; out of that death came rebirth.

The improbable source of that rebirth was a farmer named Tsali. Old Man Charley. Until October of 1838, he was simply another Indian to be herded to the stockade. A lieutenant and three other soldiers were assigned to capture all Cherokees along the headwaters of the Oconaluftee. As the patrol traveled up the Little Tennessee River, it rounded up Tsali, his family, and a few friends. The soldiers prodded the Indians with bayonets and forced Tsali's

Ginatiyun tihi, or Stephen Tehee, was born in Georgia six months before the removal of the Cherokees to the West. He served as a tribal delegate to Washington in 1898.

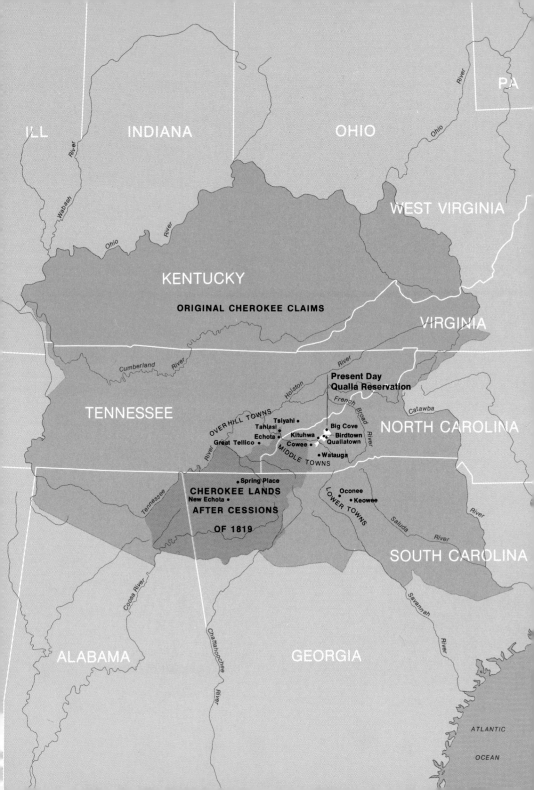

wife to hasten her steps. Driven to anger and desperation, Tsali called the other warriors to action. In the quick, sudden tangle that followed, at least one soldier was killed. Tsali and his small band fled across the river high into the Great Smoky Mountains. They hid in a massive rock shelter at the head of Deep Creek. Located on top of a steep cliff, the actual camping place lay in the midst of extensive, thick laurel and hemlock "roughs." Several hundred other Cherokees escaped from the soldiers or the stockades and found similar hiding places on the rugged, overgrown sides of the Smokies. Most of them lasted out the winter, subsisting at a near-starvation level on roots, herbs, nuts, and small game.

Tsiskwa-kaluya, or Bird Chopper, was son of Yonah-guskah, the famous Cherokee chief and spokesman who stayed with the small group in the Great Smoky Mountains.

Confronted with such determination and the likelihood of a prolonged, wearisome mission of search and arrest in the rugged mountains, General Scott offered a compromise. If Tsali and his small party would come down and give themselves up for punishment, the rest of the Cherokee fugitives would be allowed to stay in the mountains until a solution could be reached by all sides. Scott sent W. H. Thomas, a white man who had grown up with the Cherokees, into the Smokies to present the terms. Thomas found Tsali, who silently listened and decided on his own accord to accompany Thomas out of the mountains. Early in the year of 1839, Tsali and his brother and his eldest son were shot by a firing squad. The youngest son, Wasituna (for Washington) was left to take word of the deaths back to the Cherokees who remained in their hills.

They had held onto their homeland in the Great Smoky Mountains. By nothing more than the thin grip of desperate determination, they had held on, and they would remain. Reinforced by General Scott's promise, scattered friends in the East, and Thomas' political negotiations with Washington and North Carolina, the Cherokee remnant soon became the Eastern Band. Their homeland would now be known as the Qualla Reservation. So the Cherokees East, along with the white pioneers of the Great Smokies, turned together to brace the mountainous challenge of the 19th century.

From Pioneer to Mountaineer

While events of the early 19th century in the surrounding southland and the nation were moving inexorably toward conflict on bloody battlefields to decide issues which could not or would not be resolved in the political arena, people in the Great Smokies were pursuing their struggle to survive and adapt to their stern and splendid surroundings.

The early explorers, the long hunters, the initial homesteaders, the trailblazers and the groundbreakers—these had forever set a human seal upon the wilderness. Now it was the time of pioneer becoming mountaineer. Henceforth, as new settlers or curious travelers or specialized seekers in a dozen fields made their way into the mountains, they would find someone already there to welcome them.

That "someone" was becoming known by terms which might alternately serve as a source of description, derision, or definition. Highlander. Hillbilly. Mountaineer. The least offensive word was "highlander," with its overtones of the misty Scottish landscape and fierce clan loyalties from which many of the Smokies' family lines had recently descended. "Mountaineer" varied. Used to denote the proud individualism that characterized many of the stalwart men and women whose roots held deep and fast in this isolated place, "mountaineer" was a strong, acceptable name. But turned into a catchword for some picturesque, inadequate character who divided his time between the homemade dulcimer and the home-run distillery, "mountaineer" was suspect. "Hillbilly" came to verge on insult, as it conjured up cartoons of lanky, sub-human creatures who were quick to feud, slow to work, and often indifferent to the "progress" by which helpful visitors would like to transform mountain lives and attitudes.

Of course, the trouble with any single word that tried to summarize these complex and distinctive lives was its limited ability to convey more than a stereotype or a single facet. Yet the 19th and early 20th centuries saw the rise and wide adoption of such terms, with an accompanying unease—sometimes outrage—on the part of those described. This tension has persisted into the present day, for Southern Appalachian natives often have felt they have been misunderstood, or exploited, by the curious outlanders.

The visitors indeed were curious—curious about

Aaron Swaniger was an individualist who occasionally stayed in Cades Cove. To some "mountaineers" he was a "hillbilly."

Edouard E. Exline

mountain people but also about topography, altitudes, plants, wildlife, and the rich variety of natural resources abounding throughout these hills. Naturalists and botanists followed the lead of Frenchman André Michaux and Philadelphian William Bartram, who had come collecting plants in the Southern mountains during the previous century. It was Michaux who had told mountain herb-gatherers about ginseng's commercial value, and Bartram who had discovered and described the showy flame azalea brightening the spring woods.

Among 19th-century arrivals, S. B. Buckley wrote the earliest comprehensive botanical report of the Great Smokies. He marveled at that scenery, "surpassing anything we remember to have seen among the White Mountains of New Hampshire," and at the variety of flora. "Here," he wrote in the mid-1800s, "is a strange admixture of Northern and Southern species of plants, while there are quite a number which have been found in no other section of the world." Later naturalists would share his enthusiasm and enlarge on his studies.

Journalists came. One was a reporter named Charles Lanman, secretary to Daniel Webster, who rode through the hills in 1848 and wrote a book called *Letters from the Alleghany Mountains.* Through his descriptive adventures readers had a glimpse into a region more remote to their experience than many foreign countries. If the Smokies were described by him as one large upthrust, perhaps that was because he saw the range through a purple haze. He wrote at one point:

"This mountain is the loftiest of a large brotherhood which lies crowded together between North Carolina and Tennessee. Its height cannot be less than five thousand feet above the level of the sea . . . and all I can say of its panorama is that I can conceive of nothing more grand and imposing."

Lanman was only the first of many writers who would come seeking high adventure and good copy, but his lack of exactitude about the physical features of the mountains was soon to be remedied by another group of visitors. Some scientists could not be content with hunters' yarns and the poetic prose of journalists; they wanted precise facts and figures by which both native and stranger could better appreciate the landscape.

Cherokee veterans of Thomas' Legion attending a Confederate reunion in the early 1900s in New Orleans include (front from left) Young Deer, unidentified man, Pheasant, Chief David Reed, (back from left) Dickey Driver, Lt. Col. W. W. Stringfield, Lt. Suatie Owl, and Jim Keg. Stringfield was a white officer in the legion which participated with varying degrees of success in several skirmishes in the Smokies and, perhaps more importantly, which helped build the Oconaluftee Turnpike across the mountains.

One of these was Thomas Lanier Clingman, whose career included being a U.S. senator and a Confederate general as well as a scientist. A contemporary historian described him as being arrogant, aggressive, with "more than common ability" but limited scientific knowledge, whose chief service lay in arousing public curiosity in the mountains, mineralogy, and geography. He became involved in a scholarly feud with Dr. Elisha Mitchell, a transplanted Connecticut professor at the University of North Carolina, over which peak constituted the highest point east of the Mississippi River. While they were trying to settle the question, Mitchell was killed in an accidental fall on the slopes of the North Carolina pinnacle which later was given his name. Clingman's name came to grace the mountain he had explored and measured: 2,025-meter (6,643-foot)-high Clingmans Dome on the crest of the Great Smokies, only 13 meters (43 feet) lower than the lofty Mt. Mitchell.

The most fascinated and impressive visitor during these years of the mid-19th century came from another mountain terrain. Arnold Guyot, remembered today by the peak at the eastern end of the Great Smokies which bears his name, was born in Switzerland in 1807. His studies in physical geography had won him distinction throughout Europe before he came to America and accepted a chair at Princeton University in 1854. Paul Fink, a historian of the Great Smoky Mountains, has said that although forerunners of Guyot glimpsed segments of the Smokies and described certain details,

"it remained for this man of foreign birth to penetrate these mountains, spend months among them, measure their heights for the first time, and have drawn under his own direction the first map we have showing the range in detail."

Clingman secured for his friend Guyot a local guide named Robert Collins. The mountain man and the professor struggled through the roughest laurel "hells" and up the steepest slopes, measuring, calibrating, and finally naming many of the unknown heights. Guyot's journals combined precision and poetry, and they related the awesome Smokies to the human scene in ways that had not been previously possible. From that point on, natives and visitors alike could both know and appreciate more of this green homeland. But, as Paul Fink has pointed out,

"With Guyot's labors the early explorations of the Smokies ceased."

Why? What happened to cut off so abruptly the increasing flow of visitors to this virgin country? The happening was war.

The Great Smokies country, with its upland farms and small home crafts, was not in the mainstream of the decisive struggle between a plantation South and an industrial North. Nor was it in the mainstream of the violent action that convulsed its surrounding region. There had been slaves in some of the more prosperous mountain households, but few citizens in the Great Smokies area would have waged war either to defend or abolish the peculiar institution.

What some did resist was being conscripted by either side. "Scouting" became a well-used word defining a new experience in the Smokies. It applied to anyone hiding out in the hills to escape going into the Confederate or the Union army. Secretly supplied with food and clothes by their families and sympathetic friends, such "scouts" could hold out for years against the searches of outlander officials. Sometimes they did in fact become scouts, guiding escaped captives from Andersonville and other Confederate prisons through the mountains toward northern territory, and those fleeing from Yankee prisons toward their southern homes.

Many of the mountain people, of course, followed the example of their neighbors throughout the region and put on the formal uniform of blue or gray. There were sharp divisions within counties, towns, and families in the choice between state and nation. Perhaps no single section of the United States was as bitterly torn in its allegiance.

Tennessee and North Carolina had long held strong Union sentiments; but when Lincoln called for troops in the aftermath of the firing on Fort Sumter, the two states officially rallied to the Confederate cause. North Carolinians, who had been notably reluctant to leave the Union and who bristled at the injustices of "a rich man's war and a poor man's fight," nonetheless sent more men to the Confederacy than any other state. Many of these were western North Carolinians, following the leadership of their own Zebulon (Zeb) Baird Vance, born in Buncombe County and occupying the governor's chair in Raleigh during the war. Yet the fact that adjoining

Mountain women and girls had to be proficient at making many things, for there weren't many — if any — stores nearby. Over the years, Hazel Bell and many another woman spent hours and hours churning butter.

East Tennessee was overwhelmingly Union—and sent more men into the Federal forces than some of the New England states—affected the North Carolinians as well. With the two states' actual secession from the Union, numerous mountain pockets in effect seceded from their states and chose to remain loyal to the Union. Thus the little rebellion inside the larger revolt compounded the agonizing conflict of war and made every cove and community and hearthside a potential battleground.

And no matter which army the men marched with, their characteristics remained surprisingly intact. The historian of one North Carolina Confederate regiment described some of the soldiers from Haywood County:

"These mountain men had always been accustomed to independence of thought and freedom of action, and having elected for their company officers their neighbors and companions, they had no idea of surrendering more of their personal liberty than should be necessary to make them effective soldiers. Obedient while on duty and independent while off duty, this spirit to a marked degree they retained to the close of the war."

The experience of Radford Gatlin concentrated in a single episode both the sharp divisions and the ironies of war in the mountains. Gatlinburg, now a commercial and flourishing tourist mecca at the edge of the park, bears the name of a man who was driven out of that town because of his unpopular stand during the war. The sturdily built, enterprising, and somewhat arrogant Gatlin was not a man to conceal his beliefs. With his wife and a slave woman he had come from North Carolina by way of Jefferson County, Tennessee, to the community known as White Oak Flats and had established a successful general store and a less successful church: the New Hampshire Baptist Gatlinites. When Dick Reagan was appointed postmaster for a new postal service to be established in White Oak Flats in 1860, the office was located amidst the axes, guns, coffee, sugar, and bells of Gatlin's store, and Reagan renamed the post office, and therefore the town, after his good friend the storekeeper.

But when war came and Radford Gatlin not only supported the Confederacy but made heated speeches in its favor, the strongly Unionist villagers turned

against him. After being beaten by a band of masked men, Gatlin abandoned his claim to thousands of hectares that now lie within the park and departed forever from the place that was to perpetuate his name if not his memory.

The war's severest hardships followed in the wake of the outliers, or the bushwhackers. These scavengers favored no cause. As the war dragged on, they ambushed and raided, stealing meat from the smokehouse, corn from the crib, and farm animals from barn and pasture. Scarcity and want became commonplace throughout the mountains. In North Carolina's Madison County, a group of citizens broke into a warehouse and laid claim to a valuable commodity, salt. Economic want enflamed political emotions. In Tennessee's Sevier County, controversial "Parson" Brownlow, Methodist circuit-rider turned newspaper editor turned politician, sought refuge in the shadow of the Smokies with Unionist sympathizers when Knoxville came under Confederate control.

A well-known army unit operated in the Smokies: Col. William Thomas' Confederate 69th-N.C., known as Thomas' Legion of Indians and Highlanders. "Little Will," as he was affectionately called, had become the effective spokesman in Washington and at the state level for the eastern remnant of the Cherokee. When the Civil War came and he chose to stay with the South, the Cherokees chose to stay with him. For a while, they secured mineral supplies for the Confederacy, including alum and saltpeter for gunpowder. The Legion guarded Alum Cave in the Smokies. Under Thomas' direction, his unit also worked on the Oconaluftee Turnpike.

In December 1863, after Gen. Ambrose E. Burnside had secured Knoxville for the Union, Col. William J. Palmer and the 15th Pennsylvania Cavalry attacked Thomas' camp near Gatlinburg. After a short battle, Thomas and his troops retreated across the mountains into North Carolina. One month later, Confederate Gen. Robert P. Vance decided to remedy the situation in the mountains. With 375 cavalry, 100 infantry, and artillery, he marched from Asheville, joined Thomas and 150 Indian troops in Quallatown, and crossed the Smokies during a bitterly cold spell. While Thomas remained in Gatlinburg, Vance proceeded toward Newport,

Page 80: Aunt Celia Ownby cards, or straightens, wool fibers that have already been washed.

Page 81: Hettie, Martha, and Louisa Walker run cotton through a gin built by their father, John. He made the rollers out of hickory and the rest out of oak. Three people were required to operate the gin: one to feed the cotton into it and one on each end to turn each of the rollers. The ginned cotton fell into a white oak basket, also made by John Walker.

Wash day was a laborious one of lifting large buckets of water and stirring steaming kettles of dirty clothes.

Over another fire, Mrs. Kate Duckett and daughter Tennie of Coopers Creek make hard soap. Mrs. Duckett stirs the lard with a wooden paddle as Tennie fans the fire with a hawk wing before dipping into the kettle with a gourd scoop. It was a five-hour process.

camped on Cosby Creek deep in the Smokies, and was surprised there by none other than Colonel Palmer and his 15th-Pa. In the resulting rout, General Vance was captured along with about everything else: men, horses, medical supplies, food, ammunition. In February, Thomas and his Legion were engaged once more, in the Great Smoky Mountains near the mouth of Deep Creek. The result was another defeat, this time by the 14th Illinois Cavalry under Maj. Francis Davidson.

Thomas and his Legion did not win mighty military victories for the Confederacy; Governor Vance even accused Thomas' command of being "a favorite resort for deserters." But it appears that this strange little mountain force did act as a deterrent against wholesale raids in the Smokies by Federal sympathizers, and to some extent, raids by marauding bushwhackers. As for "Little Will" himself, mental disorder in later years brought him his own personal civil war and its losing battles. He died in a North Carolina hospital.

An equally well-known force in the Great Smokies during the war was a band of Union raiders led by Col. George W. Kirk. One contemporary called him "Kirk of Laurel," referring to a remote watershed in Madison County where the colonel often camped. Kirk's most effective march into the Smokies came near the close of the war, in the early spring of 1865. With 400 cavalry and 200 infantry he entered the mountains through East Tennessee's Cocke County, via Mt. Sterling, and marched into Cataloochee. Turning aside a Confederate company there, he went on to Waynesville, then proceeded to Soco Valley and back across the Smokies.

Kirk raided, released Federal prisoners, skirmished with home guards, and scattered general fear throughout the mountains. In fact, his main achievement for his cause lay in diverting Confederate troops and keeping them scattered on the home front rather than mobilized on the battlefields where they were desperately needed. Try as they might, the Confederates could not find enough of the "silver-greys" or the "seed-corn"—as those too old and too young for regular service were called—to totally protect their homeland from Kirk's men, or from renegade bushwhackers who had no cause but plunder and pillage.

As the Civil War drew toward its final convulsion, the mountain area engaged in a more familiar struggle for survival. Food was scarce, soda and salt almost non-existent. Women leached lye from wood ashes and made soda. There was no substitute for salt; when available, it cost a precious dollar a pound. Bitter enmities divided families, communities, and counties. Life had never been easy in the mountains; now it was rigorously difficult. And the people in this land of "make do or do without" learned new ways to make do. Continuing old habits and traditions up their isolated coves and along their steep hillsides, they created a life that was distinctive, rugged, and adapted to its natural surroundings.

One historian, John Preston Arthur, has described the mountain woman's day as follows:

"Long before the pallid dawn came sifting in through chink and window they were up and about. As there were no matches in those days, the housewife 'unkivered' the coals which had been smothered in ashes the night before to be kept 'alive' till morning, and with 'kindling' in one hand and a live coal held on the tines of a steel fork or between iron tongs in the other, she blew and blew and blew till the splinters caught fire. Then the fire was started and the water brought from the spring, poured into the 'kittle,' and while it was heating the chickens were fed, and cows milked, the children dressed, the bread made, the bacon fried and then coffee was made and breakfast was ready. That over and the dishes washed and put away, the spinning wheel, the loom or the reel were the next to have attention, meanwhile keeping a sharp lookout for the children, hawks, keeping the chickens out of the garden, sweeping the floor, making the beds, churning, sewing, darning, washing, ironing, taking up the ashes, and making lye, watching for the bees to swarm, keeping the cat out the milk pans, dosing the sick children, tying up the hurt fingers and toes, kissing the sore place well again, making soap, robbing the bee hives, stringing beans for winter use, working the garden, planting and tending a few hardy flowers in the front yard, such as princess feather, pansies, sweet-Williams, dahlias, morning glories; getting dinner, darning, patching, mending, milking again, reading the Bible, prayers, and so on from morning till night; and then all over again the next day."

Mrs. Clem Enloe of Tight Run Branch was 84 years old when Joseph S. Hall photographed her in 1937. "I was told that if I took her a box of snuff, she would let me take her picture." That's the snuff in her blouse. She didn't give in so easily on everything. She refused to observe the park's fishing regulations and fished every season of the year. She was filling a can with worms when Hall approached. "See that," she said pointing to the can, "I use them for fishing and I'm the only one in this park who's allowed to."

83

The one-room log school-house at Little Greenbrier, like the somewhat larger Granny's College at Big Greenbrier, provided the basics in reading, writing, and arithmetic.

And judging by the smiles of Margaret Tallent and Conley Russell, the place was lots of fun.

Herman Matthews conducts a class in the school's last year of operation, 1935. He was the only teacher who had completed college.

Emergencies of health and sickness affected the daily routines. "Doctor-medicine" might have its place, but home remedies were considered most reliable—and available. A doctor with his saddlebag of pills and tonics might be a day's ride or more away from the patient. But nature's medicine chest lay almost at the doorstep. Plants in swamp and meadow, leaves and bark and roots of the forest: all healed many ailments. From ancient Cherokee wisdom and through their own observations and testing, mountain people learned the uses of boneset, black cohosh, wild cherry, mullein, catnip, balm of gilead, Solomons-seal, sassafras, and dozens of other herbs and plants.

While they found one school and laboratory in the woods and hills around them, the people of the Great Smoky Mountains also worked to provide themselves with more orthodox classrooms. Continuing customs that had begun before the War, the residents of many little communities "made-up" a school. This meant that they banded together, and each contributed to a small fund to pay a teacher's salary for the year. The "year" was usually three months. John Preston Arthur left a vivid memoir of his experience in one of these so-called "old-field" schools, which were located on land no longer under cultivation:

"In lieu of kindergarten, graded and normal schools was the Old-Field school, of which there were generally only one or two in a county, and they were in session only when it was not 'croptime.' They were attended by little and big, old and young, sometimes by as many as a hundred, and all jammed into one room—a log cabin with a fireplace at each end—puncheon floor, slab benches, and no windows, except an opening made in the wall by cutting out a section of one of the logs, here and there. The pedagogue in charge (and no matter how large the school there was but one) prided himself upon his knowledge of and efficiency in teaching the three R's—readin', 'ritin' and 'rithmetic—and upon his ability to use effectively the rod, of which a good supply was always kept in stock. He must know, too, how to make a quill pen from the wing-feather of a goose or a turkey, steel and gold pens not having come into general use. The ink used was made from 'ink-balls' —sometimes from poke-berries—and was kept in

little slim vials partly filled with cotton. These vials, not having base enough to stand alone, were suspended on nails near the writer. The schools were paid from a public fund, the teacher boarding with the scholars."

During the latter 1800s, free schools began to replace subscription schools. But the quality and methods of education did not appear to change drastically. Across the Smokies, in East Tennessee's Big Greenbrier Cove, Granny's College provided the rudiments of public education for many students and was an example of similar schools in the Great Smokies region. Lillie Whaley Ownby remembered the house which was turned into a school:

"Granny College was built before the Civil War by Humphy John Ownby. This house was two big log houses, joined together by a huge rock chimney and a porch across both rooms on both sides of the house. The houses were built of big poplar logs. The rooms were 18x20 feet and both rooms had two doors and two windows. The floor was rough, hewn logs. There was a huge fireplace in it. The living room had a partition just behind the doors and a cellar about 8x10 feet."

After Mrs. Ownby's father had acquired the old log building, he went to Sevierville, the county seat, and proposed to the school superintendent that he would furnish this house if the county would supply a teacher for Big Greenbrier children. This was agreeable, and Granny's College, as it was locally known, came into being.

"The men made benches, long enough for three or four to sit on. The back was nailed up on some blocks and the children used the wall for a back rest. There was no place for books except on the benches or floor. Dad furnished wood for the fire. The boys carried it in and kept the fire going. Everyone helped in keeping the house clean and keeping water in the house."

Church as well as school was a personalized part of family and community life in a way not known in more formal, urban situations. Each fulfilled not only its own specific function, spiritual or intellectual, but also satisfied social needs. The doctrine was strictly fundamentalist; the dominant denominations were Baptist and Methodist, although the Presbyterian influence was also present, especially in the schools that were founded with both money and teachers drawn from other regions of the country.

Each summer, Methodist camp meetings brought families together under the long brush arbors for weeks of sociable conversation and soulful conversion. The visiting ministers' feast of oratory was matched only by the feast of victuals prepared by housewives over the campfires as they cooked and exchanged family news, quilt patterns, recipes, and "cuttings" from favorite flowers and shrubs.

Baptists were the most numerous denomination. They divided themselves into many categories, among others the Primitives, the Freewills, the Missionaries, and one small group called the Two-Seed-in-the-Spirit. Their rules were strict: no violins in church, no dancing anywhere. To be "churched," or turned out of the congregation, was heavy punishment—and not infrequent.

One aspect of church that incorporated an important feature of mountain life was its singing. In ancient Ireland and Wales songsters had been accompanied on the harp. Settlers had brought the Old Harp song book of early hymns and anthems with them from the British Isles, and on down the valleys and across the mountains into these remote byways. The notes of this music were not round but shaped, and shape, rather than placement on a staff, indicated the note. This method simplified reading the music; and as the unaccompanied, usually untrained, singers took their pitch from a leader, they proceeded in beautiful harmony, usually in a minor key.

The mournful sound of minor chords was also familiar in the ballads common throughout the hills. Death and unrequited love were their recurring themes, whether they reached back to England and the Scottish borders, as in "Lord Thomas and Fair Elender," or recounted some local contemporary affair. Beside their blazing hearths during long, lonely winter evenings, or at jolly gatherings or through lazy summer Saturday afternoons, mountain people remembered the past and recorded the present as they sang, altering and adding to the ballads which had been taught to them and which in turn would be handed on to another generation.

And among those visitors who would begin to search the mountains during the approaching 20th century, the folk song collectors and the ballad seek-

Pages 88-89: Butchering was a chore shared by nearly everyone in a family. Here, the Ogles—Earl, Horace, Collie, and Willard—butcher a hog as they get ready for a long winter.

National Park Service

ers could find here a repository of rare, pure music—much of it now forgotten even in its own homeland. The visitors would find a way of life that might seem static but which was, indeed, changing. For the early pioneers had yielded to the authentic mountaineer. His log cabin was being replaced by sash-sawn lumber in a frame house. Extensive apple orchards and corn crops yielded the basic ingredients not only for fruit and bread but for the luxuries of a brandy and whisky known also as moonshine, white lightning, Old Tanglefoot.

Hunting and fishing, which had been necessities for the first settlers, eventually turned into sport as well. Buffalo, elk, wolves, beavers, passenger pigeons, and a variety of other game disappeared early and forever, leaving only the memory of their presence in names like Buffalo Creek, Elk Mountain, Wolf Creek, Beaverdam Valley, Pigeon River. But deer, black bear, fox, raccoon and other animals remained to challenge the mountain man and his dogs. The relationship between a hunter and his hounds was something special. A dog shot or stolen could be cause for a lifelong feud. Names of individual dogs—Old Blue, Tige, Big Red—were cherished by their owners, as were certain breeds. The Plott dogs, named after the bear hunters who bred them in Haywood County's Balsam range, were famous for their tenacity and strength in hunting bear.

One of the sharpest condemnations that could be laid on a mountain man concerned the hunting dogs. An early resident of Roaring Fork above Gatlinburg was a "hard, cruel man," despised by his neighbors and in turn despising them. He had frightened children and cut a fellow "till he like to bled to death." Finally—and most devastatingly—it was agreed that "he was the type of fellow that would pizen your dog."

Livestock raising was important throughout the Great Smoky Mountains. Stock laws had not yet been passed, and rail fences were built to keep cattle, horses, hogs, or sheep *out* of gardens, fields, and yards rather than *in* pastures, pens, and feedlots. Animals roamed the fields and woods. Hogs fattened themselves on the mast of nuts and roots from the great chestnut, oak, and hickory forests; cattle grazed on the grassy balds in summertime. By mid-May, farmers in the coves and valleys had driven

In the mountains you had to work hard at being self-sufficient. And some men did better than others. One such man was Milas Messer of Cove Creek. Setting barrel staves to the hoop takes a bit of coordination, but Messer makes it look easy.

Three children look on as he works at his shaving horse on a stave. His coopering equipment includes a draw knife, crow cutter, jointing plane, stave gauge, and barrel adze.

At his blacksmith shop Messer shapes a small metal piece, one of many he turned out just to keep his farm running.

Here is Messer the tanner, scrubbing the pelt side of a hide with a scythe blade after taking it out of the vat and removing the spent bark with a long-handled strainer.

Charles S. Grossman

Salt licks are among the few remaining pieces of evidence of the great herding activity that once flourished in the Smokies. Notches were cut into logs or chiseled into rocks so the salt wouldn't be wasted as it would be if placed on the ground. The salt was good for the cattle, and the regularity of the procedure helped to keep them from becoming completely wild.

their cattle into the high places of the Smokies. Once every three weeks or so thereafter, they returned to salt and "gentle" them, thus keeping them familiar with their owners. In October, before the first snowfall, the cattle were rounded up. If the season had been good, livestock drives to near or distant markets began.

During both the roundup and the drive, livestock marks played a critical role of identification. These were devised by each farmer—and acknowledged by his neighbors—as the "brand" signifying ownership. These might be various "crops," "knicks," and "notches:" an "underbit" (a crop out of the under part of the ear), or a "topbit," or a "swallow-fork" cut in the skin below the neck, or a combination of them all. If several kinds of animals were included on a livestock drive, there was a settled rule of procedure. Cattle led the way, followed by sheep, then hogs, and finally turkeys, which were usually the first to start peering toward the sky and searching for the night's resting place.

All of these plodding, grunting, gobbling creatures were kept in order with the help of one or two good dogs. If a hunter's dogs were valuable, a livestock drover's dogs were invaluable. "Head'em," the drover called, and his dogs brought recalcitrant animals into line, nipping the slow to hurry and curious to remain orderly.

During a long day's drive to the county seat, or a several weeks' journey to the lowlands of the Carolinas or Georgia, men and beasts surged forward in a turmoil of shouting and noise, dust and mud, autumn's lingering heat and sudden chills. But on these journeys, the men left their small mountain enclaves for a brief glimpse of the larger world. They returned home not only with bolts of cloth and winter supplies of salt and coffee, but also with news and fresh experiences.

And accounts of these experiences were related in a language that was part of the mountaineer's unique heritage. That language revealed a great deal about the people; it was strong and flexible, old yet capable of change, sometimes judged "ungrammatical" but often touched with poetry. In a later century, students and collectors would come here seeking the Elizabethan words, the rhythmic cadences of this speech. It harkened back to a distant homeland.

The mountain person's "afeard" for afraid, or "poke" for paper bag, were familiar to Shakespeare. In Chaucer could be found the mountaineer's use of "holpt" for helped, and such plurals as "nestes" and "waspes." Webster confirmed that "hit" was Saxon for it, and the primary meaning of "plague" was anything troublesome or vexatious (the mountain man might well say someone was plaguing him). The habit of turning a noun into a verb often added strength to an otherwise dull sentence: "My farm will grow enough corn to bread us through the winter," or, when speaking of the heavy shoes that were brogans, "Those hunters just brogued it through the rough places."

The daily poetry and humor of the mountain language was caught in the names of places—Pretty Hollow Gap, Charlie's Bunion, Fittified Spring, Miry Ridge, Bone Valley—and in descriptive words like "hells" and "slicks" for the tangled laurel and rhododendron thickets. It was present in the familiar names of plants: "hearts-a-bustin'-with-love," "dog-hobble," "farewell summer." And the patterns of their quilts, pieced with artistic patience and skill, bore names such as "tree of life," "Bonaparte's March," and "double wedding ring."

Thus, the mountain people adapted their language, as they had their lives, to the needs and beauty of this land they called home. And contrary to what might seem the case, these later residents were a more nearly distinctive group than that which had first come. The pioneers had been a fairly heterogeneous group, but as the years passed, those with itching feet and yearning minds moved on to other frontiers. Restless children wandered west in search of instant gold and eternal youth. In time, those remaining behind became a more and more cohesive group, sharing a particular challenge, history, folklore, economy, dream. Their lives were gradually improving. They had earned the privilege and joy of calling this their homeland.

Spinning and Weaving

Like Homer's Penelope, like the Biblical spinners and weavers, like their sisters at the wheel and loom in many times and places, women of the Great Smokies simultaneously fulfilled the need for sturdy cloth and a need for creating esthetic designs and pleasing patterns. Frances Goodrich, who spent four decades helping to preserve and honor the region's handicrafts, wrote: "Hardly any other subject arouses so much enthusiasm and interest in a circle of mountain women as does the

National Park Service

National Park Service

subject of weaving and its kindred arts. This is true whether the participants in the talk are themselves weavers or only their kinsfolk. Such work has for generations taken the place of all other artistic expression, and everyone, at least in the days of which I am telling, knew something by experience or by watching the work or by hearsay and tradition, of this fine craft. . . . In the younger women who were learning to weave and keeping at it, I could see the growth of character. A slack twisted person cannot

make a success as a weaver of coverlets. Patience and perseverance are of the first necessity, and the exercise of these strengthen the fibers of the soul. . . . One who has had to do with hundreds of mountain girls . . . has told me that never did she find one to be of weak and flabby character whose mother was a weaver; there was always something in the child to build on." Turning animal and vegetable fibers into cloth necessitated several steps. The fibers had to be washed and then carded, or straightened, with

wire-toothed implements. Then the women combed the carded fibers and rolled them onto a rod called a distaff, hence the distaff side of the family. In the next step, Aunt Rhodie Abbott (below) stretches, twists, and winds the fibers with a spining wheel in Cades Cove. The women then dyed some of the yarn. In the last step, Becky Oakley (left) weaves the yarn into cloth on a loom. Then the women had to turn the cloth into clothes and other things.

The Sawmills Move In

A people and their style of life do not change drastically in one year or two years or three. The year 1900, then, does not define a time when thousands living in the Great Smokies suddenly abandoned their 19th-century ways and traditions and bounded into the modern world. Real transition would come only with the upheavals of the succeeding decades, only as a result of America's industrialization and two world wars and the arrival of a national park. Yet the beginning of a new century did inject one major new element into the lifestream of the Great Smoky Mountains: the lumber companies and their money.

The people who lived here had logged before. A man might operate a family enterprise along some hillside or in a low-lying cove, using a few strong-armed relatives or neighbors to help cut and move the choicest timber of the forest. Andy Huff, for example, established a small sawmill in Greenbrier Cove in 1898. Leander Whaley had cut yellow-poplar, buckeye, and linden from the upper cove—along Ramsey Prong—during the 1880s. These and a few other individual loggers felled the largest and most accessible of ultra-valuable woods such as cherry, ash, walnut, hickory, and the giant yellow-poplar, or "tulip tree." They used steady, slow-plodding oxen to drag the heavy logs to mill, then hauled the lumber to markets and railroads in stout-bedded wagons drawn by four mules, double-teamed.

But the virgin timber soon attracted a wider attention. In 1901, a report on the Southern Appalachians from President Theodore Roosevelt to Congress concluded simply that "These are the heaviest and most beautiful hard-wood forests of the continent." Of the Great Smokies in particular, the report noted that besides the hardwoods the forest contained "the finest and largest bodies of spruce in the Southern Appalachians." Lumber entrepreneurs were equally impressed. In that same year, three partners paid about $9.70 per hectare for the 34,400-hectare ($3/85,000-acre) bulk of the Little River watershed. Some 20 years later, Col. W. B. Townsend moved from Pennsylvania and took control of Little River Lumber Company.

On the North Carolina slopes of the Smokies, companies purchased land in swaths stretching from ridge to ridge, staking off watersheds like so many

In some places the Little River Lumber Company, and other logging firms, sent logs cascading down the mountain sides in intricately constructed chutes.

Little River Lumber Company

claims. In 1903, W. M. Ritter Lumber Company set up its operations along Hazel Creek. A year later, Montvale Lumber Company moved into the adjacent Eagle Creek area. To the west of Montvale would, in time, lie the Kitchin mill and its Twentymile Creek domain; to the east of Ritter, Norwood Lumber Company embraced the reaches of Forney Creek. And looming beside and above them all stood the 36,400 timbered hectares (90,000 acres) of the Champion Coated Paper Company, an area that included Deep Creek and Greenbrier Cove and the headwaters of the Oconaluftee River.

The companies needed men to cut the trees, skid the logs, work the animals, saw the lumber, lay the roads. They called upon the mountaineers who still owned small tracts in Cades Cove and Cataloochee and lower Greenbrier and throughout the Smokies; or they allowed some workers who had sold forested land to stay in their homes, though now on company property; or they brought in hired hands from outside and housed them and their families in dormitory-like buildings and readymade "towns." These mushrooming mill villages—Elkmont on the Little River, Crestmont on Big Creek, Proctor on Hazel Creek, Ravensford and Smokemont and Fontana—provided a booming cash market for homegrown food and, as soon as the money changed hands, imported products.

More often than not, residents of the Great Smoky Mountains drove to and from market in covered wagons that protected their goods. Because the drive to an outside market such as Waynesville, Newport, or Maryville might take two or even three days, local families sold what they could to the loggers and sawmill men. They set up honey and apple stands along the roads and offered grapes in season. They supplied stores with butter and eggs. Children could trade in one egg for a week's supply of candy or firecrackers.

A businesslike atmosphere filtered through the quiet of the Smokies. Though wolves and panthers had largely disappeared by 1910, fur buyers and community traders enjoyed a brisk exchange in mink, raccoon, fox, and 'possum hides. Oak bark and chestnut wood, called "tanbark" and "acid wood" because they were sources of valuable tannic acid, brought $7 per cord when shipped to Asheville or Knoxville. As the sawmills flourished, makeshift box houses of vertical poplar and chestnut planks gave way to more substantial weatherboarded homes of horizontal lengths and tight-fitting frames. Slick, fancy, buggy-riding "drummers" peddled high-button shoes and off-color stories. The spacious Wonderland Park Hotel and the Appalachian Club at Elkmont, and a hunting lodge on Jake's Creek graced the once forbidding mountainsides.

Undergirding this development was a growing cash base: peaches and chestnuts, pork and venison, wax and lard—translated into money—brought flour and sugar, yarn and needles, tools and ammunition. Yet in the midst of this new-found activity, many clung to their old habits. Children still found playtime fun by sliding down hills of pine needles and "riding" poplar saplings from treetop to treetop. Hard-shell Baptist preachers, such as the hunter and "wilderness saddle-bagger" known as "Preacher John" Stinnett, still devoted long spare hours, and sometimes workdays as well, to reading The Book: "I just toted my Bible in a tow sack at the handle of my bull tongue and I studied it at the turn of the furrow and considered it through the rows."

But whatever the immediate considerations of the hour happened to be, logging was the order of the day. From the Big Pigeon River, all the way to the Little Tennessee, the second generation of timber-cutters had moved into the Smokies on a grand scale.

The companies, with their manpower, their strategically placed sawmills, and their sophisticated equipment, produced board feet of lumber by the millions. The rest of the country, with its increased demands for paper and residential construction, absorbed these millions and cried for more. By 1909, when production attained its peak in the Smokies and throughout the Appalachians, logging techniques had reached such an advanced state that even remote stands of spruce and hemlock could be worked with relative ease. Demand continued unabated and even received a slight boost when World War I broke out in 1914.

High volume covered high costs. The Little River Lumber Company, perhaps the most elaborate logging operation in the Smokies, cut a total of two billion board feet. Cherry, the most valuable of the

Pages 100-101: Sawmills, such as this one at Lawson's Sugar Cove, were quickly set up in one location and just as quickly moved to another as soon as the plot was cleared.

woods, with its exquisite grain and rich color, was also the scarcest. Yellow-poplar, that tall, straight tree with a buoyancy that allowed it to float high, turned out to be the most profitable of all saw timber. Coniferous forests, the thick, dark regions of pungent spruce and hemlock, yielded a portion of the company's output.

Extraction of such proportions was not easy. Timber cruisers combed the forests, estimating board feet and ax-marking suitable trees. Three-man saw teams followed the cruisers. One, the "chipper," calculated the fall of the tree and cut a "lead" in the appropriate side. Two sawyers then took over, straining back and forth upon their crosscut saw until gravity and the immense weight of the tree finished their job for them. The work was hard and hazardous. Sometimes, if the lead were not cut properly, the trunk would fall toward the men; sudden death or permanent injury might result from the kickback of a doomed tree's final crash, or from a moment's carelessness.

To remove the felled timber, larger companies laid railroad tracks far up the creeks from their mills. At the eastern edge of the Smokies, for instance, one such terminus grew into the village of Crestmont, which boasted a hotel, two movie theaters, and a well-stocked commissary. Such accommodations seemed a distant cry indeed from the upper branches of Big Creek, gathering its waters along the slopes of Mt. Sterling, Mt. Cammerer, and Mt. Guyot. Workers from improbable distances—even countries "across the waters," such as Italy—teamed with the mountain people to push a standard gauge track alongside the boulder-strewn streams. Bolted onto oaken ties that were spaced far enough apart to discourage foot travel, the black rails drove ahead, switched back to higher ground, crossed Big Creek a dozen times before they reached the flat way station of Walnut Bottoms.

Dominated by powerful, blunt-bodied locomotives, the railroads gave rise to stories that were a flavorful blend of pathos and danger. "Daddy" Bryson and a fireman named Forrester were killed on a sharp curve along Jake's Creek of Little River. Although Forrester jumped clear when the brakes failed to hold, he was buried under an avalanche of deadly, cascading logs. There were moments of comedy as well as tragedy. In the same river basin, Colonel Townsend asked engineer Noah Bunyan Whitehead one day when he was going to stop putting up all that black smoke from his train. Bun answered: "When they start making white coal."

Railroads could reach only so far, however. The most complex phase of the logging process was "skidding," or bringing the felled logs from inaccessible distances to the waiting cars. As the first step, men armed with cant hooks or short, harpoon-like peavies, simply rolled the logs down the mountainsides. Such continuous "ball-hooting," as it was called, gouged paths which rain and snow etched deeper into scars of heavy erosion. Sometimes oxen and mules pulled, or "snaked," the timber through rough terrain to its flatcar destination. Horses soon replaced the slower animals and proved especially adept at "jayhooking," or dragging logs down steep slopes by means of J-hooks and grabs. When the logs gained speed and threatened to overtake them, the men and nimble-footed horses simply stepped onto a spur trail; the open link slipped off at the J-hook and the logs slid on down the slope under their own momentum.

Even more ingenious skidding methods were devised. Splash-dams of vertical hemlock boards created reservoirs on otherwise shallow, narrow streams. The released reservoir, when combined with heavy rains, could carry a large amount of timber far downstream. In the mill pond, loggers with hobnailed boots kept the logs moving and uncorked occasional jams. Another method devised to move virgin timber down steep slopes was the trestled flume. The large, wooden graded flumes provided a rapid but expensive mode of delivery. One carried spruce off Clingmans Dome.

There were, finally, the loader and skidders. The railroad-mounted steam loader was nicknamed the "Sarah Parker" after "a lady who must have been real strong." The skidder's revolving drum pulled in logs by spectacular overhead cables. Loaded with massive timber lengths, these cables spanned valleys and retrieved logs from the very mountaintops.

To coordinate all of these operations efficiently required skill and judgment. The lumber companies devised numerous approaches to the problem of maximum production at lowest cost. They con-

Massive steam-powered skidders pulled logs in off the hills to a central pile. Then the loaders took over and put the logs on trains, which carried them to the mills.

tracted with individuals; Andy Huff, for example, continued to run a mill at the mouth of Roaring Fork and paid his men a full 75 cents for a 16-hour day. The corporations sometimes worked together; in one maneuver, Little River helped Champion flume its spruce pulpwood to the Little River railroad for shipment to Champion's paper mill at Canton, North Carolina. Haste and carelessness could lead to shocking waste. When one company moved its operations during World War I, 1.5 million board feet of newly cut timber was left to rot at the head of Big Creek.

The ravages of logging led to fires. Although fires were sometimes set on purpose to kill snakes and insects and to burn underbrush, abnormal conditions invited abnormal mishaps. Parched soil no longer held in place by a web of living roots, dry tops of trees piled where they had been flung after trimming the logs, and flaming sparks of locomotives or skidders: any combination of these caused more than 20 disastrous fires in the Smokies during the 1920s. A two-month series of fires devastated parts of Clingmans Dome, Siler's Bald, and Mt. Guyot. One holocaust on Forney Creek, ignited by an engine spark, raced through the tops of 24-meter (80-foot) hemlocks and surged over 5 kilometers (3 miles) in four hours. A site of most intense destruction was in the Sawtooth range of the Charlie's Bunion area.

Despite the ravages of fire, erosion, and the voracious ax and saw, all was not lost. Some two-thirds of the Great Smoky Mountains was heavily logged or burned, but pockets of virgin timber remained in a shrinking number of isolated spots and patches at the head of Cataloochee, the head of Greenbrier, and much of Cosby and Deep Creek. And as the 1920s passed into another decade, the vision of saving what was left of this virgin forest, saving the land—saving the homeland—grew in the lonely but insistent conscience of a small number of concerned and convincing citizens.

George Washington Shults and some neighbors snake out large trunks with the help of six oxen. Sometimes the lumber companies would hire such local people to handle a specific part of the operation. Today we call the process subcontracting.

Of the many kinds of trees logged in the Great Smokies, the largest and most profitable were the yellow-poplars, more commonly known as tulip trees. A man could feel pretty small standing next to one of them.

The great scale of the logging machinery was like nothing the Smokies had seen before. Long trains carried loads of huge tree trunks to sawmills after the flat cars were loaded by railroad-mounted cranes.

Birth of a Park

Logging dominated the life of the Great Smoky Mountains during the early decades of the 20th century. But there was another side to that life. Apart from the sawmills and the railroads and the general stores, which were bustling harbingers of new ways a-coming, the higher forests, the foot trails, and the moonshine stills remained as tokens of old ways a-lingering. One person in particular came to know and speak for this more primitive world.

Horace Kephart was born in 1862 in East Salem, Pennsylvania. His Swiss ancestors were pioneers of the Pennsylvania frontier. During his childhood, Kephart's family moved to the Iowa prairie, where his mother gave him a copy of the novel *Robinson Crusoe* by Daniel Defoe. In the absence of playmates on the vast Midwest grassland, young Kephart dreamed and invented his own games, fashioned his own play swords and pistols out of wood and even built a cave out of prairie sod and filled it with "booty" collected off the surrounding countryside.

Horace Kephart never forgot his frontier beginnings. He saved his copy of *Robinson Crusoe* and added others: *The Wild Foods of Great Britain, The Secrets of Polar Travel,* Theodore Roosevelt's *The Winning of the West.* Camping and outdoor cooking, ballistics and photography captured his attention and careful study.

Kephart polished his education with periods of learning and library work at Boston University, Cornell, and Yale. In 1887 he married a girl from Ithaca, New York, and began to raise a family. By 1890, he was librarian of the well-known St. Louis Mercantile Library. In his late thirties, Kephart grew into a quiet, intense loner, a shy and reticent man with dark, piercing eyes. He remained an explorer at heart, a pioneer, an individual secretly nurturing the hope of further adventures.

Opportunity arrived in a strange disguise. Horace Kephart's largely unfulfilled visions of escape were combined with increasingly prolonged periods of drinking. Experience with a tornado in the streets of St. Louis affected his nerves. As he later recalled:

"*. . . then came catastrophe; my health broke down. In the summer of 1904, finding that I must abandon professional work and city life, I came to western North Carolina, looking for a big primitive forest where I could build up strength anew and indulge*

Conducting a preliminary survey of the park's boundaries in 1931 are (from left) Superintendent J. Ross Eakin, Arthur P. Miller, Charles E. Peterson, O. G. Taylor, and John Needham.

George A. Grant

George Masa

Horace Kephart, librarian-turned-mountaineer, won the hearts of the Smokies people with his quiet and unassuming ways. He played a major role in the initial movement for a national park.

my lifelong fondness for hunting, fishing and exploring new ground."

He chose the Great Smokies almost by accident. Using maps and a compass while he rested at his father's home in Dayton, Ohio, he located the nearest wilderness and then determined the most remote corner of that wilderness. After his recuperation he traveled to Asheville, North Carolina, where he took a railroad line that wound through a honeycomb of hills to the small way station of Dillsboro. And from there, at the age of 42, he struck out, with a gun and a fishing rod and three days' rations, for the virgin mountainside forest. After camping for a time on Dick's Creek, his eventual wild destination turned out to be a deserted log cabin on the Little Fork of the Sugar Fork of Hazel Creek.

His nearest neighbors lived 3 kilometers (2 miles) away, in the equally isolated settlement of Medlin. Medlin consisted of a post office, a corn mill, two stores, four dwellings, and a nearby schoolhouse that doubled as a church. The 42 households that officially collected their mail at the Medlin Post Office inhabited an area of 42 square kilometers (16 square miles). It was, as Kephart describes it:

"... the forest primeval, where roamed some sparse herds of cattle, razorback hogs and the wild beasts. Speckled trout were in all the streams. Bears sometimes raided the fields and wildcats were a common nuisance. Our settlement was a mere slash in the vast woodland that encompassed it."

But it was also, for Horace Kephart, a new and invigorating home. He loved it. He thrived in it. At first he concentrated his senses on the natural beauty around him, on the purple rhododendron, the flame azalea, the fringed orchis, the crystal clear streams. Yet as the months passed, he found that he could not overlook the people.

The mountain people were as solidly a part of the Smokies as the boulders themselves. These residents of branch and cove, of Medlin and Proctor and all the other tiny settlements tucked high along the slanting creekbeds of the Great Smoky Mountains, these distinctive "back of beyond" hillside farmers and work-worn wives and wary moonshine distillers lodged in Kephart's consciousness and imagination with rock-like strength and endurance.

Initially silent and suspicious of this stranger in

their midst, families gradually came to accept him. They approved of his quietness and his even-handed ways, even confiding in him with a simple eloquence. One foot-weary distiller, after leading Kephart over kilometers of rugged terrain, concluded: "Everywhere you go, it's climb, scramble, clamber down, and climb again. You cain't go nowheres in this country without climbin' both ways." The head of a large family embracing children who spilled forth from every corner of the cabin confessed: "We're so poor, if free silver was shipped in by the carload we couldn't pay the freight."

Kephart came to respect and to wonder at these neighbors who combined a lack of formal education with a fullness of informal ability. Like him, many of their personal characters blended a weakness for liquor with a strong sense of individual etiquette. He heard, for example, the story of an overnight visitor who laid his loaded gun under his pillow; when he awoke the next morning, the pistol was where he had left it, but the cartridges stood in a row on a nearby table.

He met one George Brooks of Medlin: farmer, teamster, storekeeper, veterinarian, magistrate, dentist. While Brooks did own a set of toothpullers and wielded them mercilessly, some individuals practiced the painful art of tooth-jumping to achieve the same result. Uncle Neddy Carter even tried to jump one of his own teeth; he cut around the gum, wedged a nail in, and made ready to strike the nail with a hammer, but he missed the nail and mashed his nose instead.

None of these fascinating tales escaped the attention of Horace Kephart. As he regained his health, the sustained energy of his probing mind also returned. Keeping a detailed journal of his experiences, he drove himself as he had done in the past. He developed almost an obsession to record all that he learned, to know this place and people completely, to stop time for an interval and capture this mountain way of life in his mind and memory. For three years he lived by the side of Hazel Creek. Though he later moved down to Bryson City during the winters, he spent most of his summers 13 kilometers (8 miles) up Deep Creek at an old cabin that marked the original Bryson Place.

Kephart distilled much of what he learned into a

Wiley Oakley, his wife, and children gather on the porch of their Scratch Britches home at Cherokee Orchard with "Minnehaha." Oakley always said, "I have two women: one I talk to and one who talks to me."

Oakley was a park guide before there was a park. And in that role he nearly always wore a red plaid shirt. He developed friendships with Henry Ford and John D. Rockefeller and became known as the "Will Rogers of the Smokies."

series of books. *The Book of Camping and Woodcraft* appeared in 1906 as one of the first detailed guidebooks to woodsmanship, first aid, and the art we now call "backpacking," all based on his personal experience and knowledge. There is even a chapter on tanning pelts. But the most authoritative book concerned the people themselves. *Our Southern Highlanders,* published in 1913 and revised nine years later, faithfully retraces Kephart's life among the Appalachian mountain folk after he "left the tame West and came into this wild East." And paramount among the wilds of the East was the alluring saga of the moonshiner.

In Horace Kephart's own eyes, his greatest education came from the spirited breed of mountain man known as "blockade runners" or simply "blockaders." These descendants of hard-drinking Scotsmen and Irishmen had always liked to "still" a little corn whisky to drink and, on occasion, to sell. But as the 1920s opened into the era of Prohibition, the mountain distiller of a now contraband product reached his heyday. He found and began to supply an expanding, and increasingly thirsty market.

Stealth became the keynote in this flourishing industry. Mountaineers searched out laurel-strangled hollows and streams that seemed remote even to their keen eyes. There they assembled the copper stills into which they poured a fermented concoction of cornmeal, rye, and yeast known as "sour mash" or "beer." By twice heating the beer and condensing its vapors through a water-cooled "worm" or spiral tube, they could approximate the uncolored liquor enjoyed at the finest New York parties. And by defending themselves with shotguns rather than with words, they could continue their approximations.

In this uniquely romantic business, colorful characters abounded on both sides of the law. Horace Kephart wrote about a particular pair of men who represented the two legal extremes: the famous moonshiner Aquilla Rose, and the equally resilient revenuer from the Internal Revenue Service, W. W. Thomason.

Aquilla, or "Quill," Rose lived for 25 years at the head of sparsely populated Eagle Creek. After killing a man in self-defense and hiding out in Texas awhile, Rose returned to the Smokies with his wife and settled so far up Eagle Creek that he crowded

111

Aquilla Rose stands proudly with his mowing machine outside his home near Eagle Creek. He didn't stand that still when revenuers came around.

the Tennessee-North Carolina state line. Quill made whisky by the barrel and seemed to drink it the same way, although he was occasionally seen playing his fiddle or sitting on the porch with his long beard flowing and his Winchester resting across his lap. His eleventh Commandment, to "never get ketched," was faithfully observed, and Quill Rose remained one of the few mountain blockaders to successfully combine a peaceable existence at home with a dangerous livelihood up the creek.

W.W. Thomason visited Horace Kephart at Bryson City in 1919. Kephart accepted this "sturdy, dark-eyed stranger" as simply a tourist interested in the moonshining art. While Thomason professed innocence, his real purpose in the Smokies was to destroy stills which settlers were operating on Cherokee lands to evade the local law. He prepared for the job by taking three days to carve and paint a lifelike rattlesnake onto a thick sourwood club. During the following weeks, he would startle many a moonshiner by thrusting the stick close and twisting it closer.

When Kephart led the "Snake-Stick Man" into whiskyed coves in the Sugarlands or above the Cherokee reservation, he found himself deputized and a participant in the ensuing encounters. More often than not, shots rang out above the secluded thickets. In one of these shootouts, Thomason's hatband, solidly woven out of hundreds of strands of horsehair, saved this fearless revenuer's life.

All the wonders of the Great Smoky Mountains— the nature, the people, the stories, and the battles and the jests—affected Horace Kephart mightily. This man whose own life had been "saved" by the Smokies began to think in terms of repaying this mountain area in kind. For during his years on Hazel Creek and Deep Creek and in Bryson City, he saw the results of the "loggers' steel," results that caused him to lament in a single phrase, "slash, crash, go the devastating forces." In 1923 he summarized his feelings about the lumber industry:

"When I first came into the Smokies the whole region was one superb forest primeval. I lived for several years in the heart of it. My sylvan studio spread over mountain after mountain, seemingly without end, and it was always clean and fragrant, always vital, growing new shapes of beauty from day to day. The

112

When the Civilian Conservation Corps moved into the Smokies in the 1930s, young men from the cities saw moonshine stills firsthand. Here one pretends to be a moonshiner and hangs his head low for the photographer.

Grace Newman sits enraptured as Jim Proffit plays the guitar.

vast trees met overhead like cathedral roofs. . . . Not long ago I went to that same place again. It was wrecked, ruined, desecrated, turned into a thousand rubbish heaps, utterly vile and mean."

Kephart began to think in terms of a national park. He and a Japanese photographer friend, George Masa, trekked the Smokies and gathered concrete experience and evidence of the mountains' wild splendor. At every opportunity, Kephart advocated the park idea in newspapers, in brochures, and by word of mouth. He proudly acknowledged that "I owe my life to these mountains and I want them preserved that others may profit by them as I have."

The concept of a national park for these southern mountains was not a new one in 1920. Forty years earlier, a retired minister and former state geologist, Drayton Smith, of Franklin, North Carolina, had proposed "a national park in the mountains." In 1885, Dr. Henry O. Marcy of Boston, Massachusetts, had discussed future health resorts in America and had considered "the advisability of securing under state control a large reservation of the higher range as a park." By the turn of the century, the Appalachian National Park Association was formed in Asheville, North Carolina, and publicized the idea of a national park somewhere in the region, not specifically the Great Smokies. When the Federal Government seemed to rule out this possibility, the Association devoted the bulk of its time and effort to the creation of national forest reserves.

But people like Horace Kephart knew the difference between a national park that safeguarded trees and a national forest that allowed logging. In 1923, a group supporting a genuine Great Smokies park formed in Knoxville, Tennessee. Mr. and Mrs. Willis P. Davis, of the Knoxville Iron Company, in the summer of that year had enjoyed a trip to some of the country's western parks. As they viewed the wonders preserved therein, Mrs. Davis was reminded of the natural magnificence near her own home. "Why can't we have a national park in the Great Smokies?" she asked her husband.

Back in Knoxville, Mr. Davis began to ask that question of friends and associates. One of these was Col. David C. Chapman, a wholesale druggist, who listened but did not heed right away:

"Not until I accidentally saw a copy of President

Theodore Roosevelt's report on the Southern Appalachians did I have any idea of just what we have here. In reading and rereading this report I learned for the first time that the Great Smokies have some truly superlative qualities. After that I became keenly interested in Mr. Davis' plan and realized that a national park should be a possibility."

The Davises and Chapman led the formation of the Great Smoky Mountains Conservation Association. Congressmen and Secretary of the Interior Hubert Work were contacted. Work endorsed the project, and two years later Congress passed an act authorizing associations in Tennessee and North Carolina to buy lands and deed them to the U.S. Government.

Problems immediately presented themselves. The citizens would have to buy this park. Unlike Yellowstone and other previous land grants from the Federal Government, the Smokies were owned by many private interests and therefore presented a giant challenge to hopeful fund raisers. To further complicate matters, no group had the power to condemn lands; any property, if secured at all, would have to be coaxed from its owner at an appropriately high price. Finally, and most discouragingly, park enthusiasts faced an area of more than 6,600 separate tracts and thousands of landowners.

Yet events conspired to give the park movement a sustaining drive. The lumber companies had made the people of the Smokies more dependent on money for additional food, modern-day clothing, and new forms of recreation. World War I and the coming of the highways had instilled a restlessness in the mountain people, a yearning for new sights and different ways of living. Some began to echo the sentiments of one farmer who, after realizing meager returns for his hard labor on rocky fields, looked around him and concluded, "Well, I reckon a park is about all this land is fit for."

Determined leadership overcame obstacles large and small. Behind Chapman's professorial appearance —his wire-rimmed glasses and three-piece suits and unkempt hair—was a man who had been a colonel in World War I, a man who had resolved to make the dream of a national park into a reality. Along with Chapman as the driving force, associate director of the National Park Service Arno B. Cammerer provided the steering and the gears. Cammerer's marked enthusiasm for incorporating the Great Smokies into the national park system added a well-placed, influential spokesman to the movement. By spring of 1926, groups in North Carolina and Tennessee had raised more than a million dollars. Within another year, the legislatures of the two states each had donated twice that amount.

With $5 million as a nest egg, park advocates turned to the actual buying of lands. Cammerer himself defined a boundary which included the most suitable territory and which, as it turned out, conformed closely to the final boundary. Chapman and his associates approached individual home-owners. Sometimes they received greetings similar to one on a homemade sign:

"Col. Chapman. You and Hoast are notify. Let the Cove People Alone. Get Out. Get Gone. 40 m. Limit."

The older mountain people clung desperately to what they had. Even though the buyers were prepared to issue lifetime leases for those who wanted to stay, they found it difficult to remove this resolute band from their homeland.

Many of the Smokies' residents—the younger, more mobile, more financially oriented ones— accepted the coming of the park with a combination of fatalism and cautious hope. Gradually they acknowledged the fact that a park and its tourist trade might be a continuing asset, whereas the prosperity from logging had proved at best only temporary. After John D. Rockefeller, Jr., through the Laura Spelman Rockefeller Memorial Fund, doubled the park fund with a much-needed gift of an additional $5 million, renewed offers of cash completely melted many icy objections.

The lumber companies followed suit, but for higher stakes. Champion Fibre, Little River, Suncrest, Norwood, and Ritter were among the 18 timber and pulpwood companies that owned more than 85 percent of the proposed park area. They fought to stay for obvious economic reasons, yet they were prepared to leave if the price was right. Little River Lumber Company, after considerable negotiation with the state of Tennessee and the city of Knoxville, sold its 30,345 hectares (75,000 acres) for only $8.80 per hectare ($3.57 per acre).

The vast holdings of Champion Fibre Company were at the very heart of the park, however, and the results of the company's resistance to a national park were central to success or failure of the whole movement. Champion's 36,400 hectares (90,000 acres) included upper Greenbrier, Mt. Guyot, Mt. LeConte, the Chimneys, and a side of Clingmans Dome, crowned by extensive forests of virgin spruce. This splendid domain was the cause of hot tempers, torrid accusations, rigid defenses, and a hard-fought condemnation lawsuit. In the end, however, on March 30, 1931, Champion Fibre agreed to sell for a total of $3 million, a sum which took on added appeal during the slump of the disastrous Depression.

Four days after this agreement, Horace Kephart died in an automobile accident near Cherokee, North Carolina. An 8-ton boulder was later brought from the hills above Smokemont to mark his grave in Bryson City.

Only a few years earlier Kephart had said:

"Here to-day is the last stand of primeval American forest at its best. If saved—and if saved at all it must be done at once—it will be a joy and a wonder to our people for all time. The nation is summoned by a solemn duty to preserve it."

And it was, indeed, preserved. The Federal Government in 1933 contributed a final $2 million to the cause, establishing the figure of $12 million as the grand total of money raised for the park. On September 2, 1940, with land acquisition almost completed, President Franklin D. Roosevelt dedicated the Great Smoky Mountains National Park "for the permanent enjoyment of the people."

The park movement's greatest victory, coming as it did at Kephart's death, lent a special significance to his life. For his experience symbolized the good effects that a national park in the Great Smoky Mountains could create. These mountains and their people inspired him to write eloquently of their truth and endurance; his own health seemed to thrive in the rugged, elemental environment of the Smokies. Perhaps most important of all, he discovered here the impact of what it can mean to know a real home. Having found a home for himself, he labored tirelessly for a national park to give to his fellow countrymen the same opportunity for wonder and renewal and growth.

An early morning fog cloaks the dense vegetation and rolling hills at Cove Creek Gap. Such scenes inspired many people to rally around the idea of purchasing land for a park.

Those attending a meeting March 6, 1928, when a $5 million gift from the Laura Spelman Rockefeller Memorial was announced, included (front from left) former Tennessee Gov. Ben W. Hooper, Willis P. Davis, E. E. Conner, David C. Chapman, Gov. Henry H. Horton, John Nolan, Knoxville Mayor James A. Fowler, (back from left) Kenneth Chorley, Arno B. Cammerer, Wiley Brownlee, J. M. Clark, Margaret Preston, Ben A. Morton, Frank Maloney, Cary Spence, and Russell Hanlon.

The Past Becomes Present

As early as 1930, citizens and officials across the United States had begun to realize that a new additional park would indeed encompass and preserve the Great Smoky Mountains. Hard-working Maj. J. Ross Eakin, the first superintendent of the park, arrived at the beginning of the next year from his previous post in Montana's Glacier National Park and was quickly introduced to the cold, mid-January winds of the Great Smokies and some of the controversies that had arisen during establishment of the park.

At first, Eakin and his few assistants limited their duties to the basics; they marked boundaries, prevented hunting, fought and forestalled fire. But as the months passed, as the park grew in size and its staff increased in number, minds and muscles alike tackled the real problem of shaping a sanctuary which all the people of present and future generations could enjoy.

Help came from an unexpected quarter. The economic depression that had gripped the country in 1930 tightened its stranglehold as the decade progressed. In the famous "Hundred Days" spring of 1933, a special session of Congress passed the first and most sweeping series of President Roosevelt's New Deal legislation. The Civilian Conservation Corps, created in April, established work for more than two million young men. CCC camps, paying $30 a month for work in conservation, flood control, and wilderness projects, sprang up.

As far as the young, struggling Great Smoky Mountains National Park was concerned, this new CCC program could not have come at a better time. Through the Corps, much-needed manpower converged by the hundreds on the Smokies from such places as New Jersey, Ohio, and New York City. Supervised by Park Service officials and reserve officers from the U.S. Army, college-age men first set up their own camps—17 in all—and then went about that old familiar labor in the Smokies, landscaping and building roads. In addition, they constructed trails, shelters, powerlines, fire towers, and bridges.

Some of their tent-strewn camps were pitched on old logging sites with familiar names like Smokemont and Big Creek. Others, such as Camp No. 413 on Forney Creek, were more remote but no less adequate. Ingenuity, sparked by necessity, created

John Walker, the patriarch of a large self-reliant family, admires cherries he raised at his home in Little Greenbrier.

Jim Shelton

accommodations which made full use of all available resources. At Camp Forney, for instance, there was a barracks, a messhall, a bathhouse, and an officers' quarters. Water from clear, cold Forney Creek was piped into the kitchen; food was stored in a home-made ice chest. The residents of the camp, seeing no reason why they should rough it more than necessary, added a library, a post office, and a commissary in their spare time.

The CCC men, their ages between 18 and 25, did not forget recreation. As teams organized for football, baseball, boxing, wrestling, and soccer, the hills resounded with unfamiliar calls of scores and umpires' decisions, while the more familiar tussles of boxing and wrestling raised echoes of old partisan matches throughout the hills. At times, these young workers answered the urge to ramble, too. One of them later recalled his days as a radio man on the top of Mt. Sterling:

"It was seven miles steep up there, and sometimes I'd jog down about sundown and catch a truck for Newport. That's where we went to be with people. The last truck brought us back after midnight."

A minor problem sometimes arose when the CCC "outsiders" began dating local girls; farming fathers sometimes set fires to give the boys something else to do during the weekends. The conflict of cultures was thrown into a particularly sharp light when a Corps participant shot a farmer's hog one night and shouted that he had killed a bear!

On the whole, however, the Civilian Conservation Corps program in the Great Smoky Mountains was a major success. In one or two extremely rugged areas of the park, retired loggers were hired in 10-day shifts to hack out or even drill short trail lengths. The rest of the 965-kilometer (600-mile) trail system, together with half a dozen fire towers and almost 480 kilometers (300 miles) of fire roads and tourist highways, was the product of the CCC. When Super-intendent Eakin evaluated the work of only the first two years of the CCC's operation, he equated it with a decade of normal accomplishment.

Through these and similar efforts, which included almost 110 kilometers (70 miles) of the famous Appalachian Trail, the natural value of the Great Smoky Mountains became a recognized and established lure for thousands, eventually millions, of visitors. But there was another resource that remained untapped, a challenge to the national park purpose and imagination. This resource was first overlooked, then neglected, and finally confronted with respect. The resource was the people and their homes.

Many previous owners of park land had received lifetime leases that allowed them to live on in their dwellings, work their fields, and cut dead timber even while tourists streamed through the Smokies. Some of the lessees, such as those living near Gatlinburg, saw a new era coming, thrusting back the street-ends until motels and restaurants and craft shops pushed against an abandoned apple orchard or a 10-plot cemetery or a deserted backyard laced with lilacs. These rememberers of an earlier time relinquished their lands in the park, more often than not resettling within sight of the mountain range and the homeland they had just left.

Yet a few lessees, those living further up the valleys, deeper into the mountains, or isolated from the well-traveled paths, these few folks stayed on. The Walker sisters of Little Greenbrier Cove were representative of this small group.

John Walker, their father, was himself the eldest of his parents' 15 children. In 1860, at the age of 19, he became engaged to 14-year-old Margaret Jane King. The Civil War postponed their wedding, and John, an ardent Unionist who had enlisted in the First Tennessee Light Artillery, spent three months in a Confederate prison and lost 45 kilograms (100 pounds) before he was exchanged and provided with a pension. In 1866, they were finally married. After Margaret Jane's father died, the young couple moved into the King homestead in Little Greenbrier.

They had eleven children: four boys, seven girls. John remained a strong Republican and Primitive Baptist; he liked to boast that in a long and fruitful lifetime he had spent a total of 50 cents on health care for his family (two of his sons had once required medicine for the measles). Margaret Jane was herself an "herb doctor" and a midwife, talents which complemented John's skills as a blacksmith, carpenter, miller, farmer. Once, as Margaret Jane was chasing a weasel from her hens, the reddish-brown animal bit her thumb and held on; she calmly thrust her hand into a full washtub, where the weasel drowned in water stained by her blood.

Columbus "Clum" Cardwell of Hills Creek, Tennessee, worked in the CCC garage at Smokemont. That experience led to a 23-year career as an auto-mechanic at the national park.

123

The children grew up. The three older boys married and moved away. The youngest, Giles Daniel, left for Iowa and fought in World War I. Sarah Caroline, the only one of the daughters ever to marry, began her life with Jim Shelton in 1908. Hettie Rebecca worked for a year or two in a Knoxville hosiery mill, but the Depression sent her back home. When Nancy Melinda died in 1931, the original home place was left in the hands of five sisters; Hettie, Margaret Jane, Polly, Louisa Susan, and Martha Ann.

They lived the self-sufficiency of their ancestors. They stated simply that "our land produces everything we need except sugar, soda, coffee, and salt." Their supplies came from the grape arbor, the orchard, the herb and vegetable garden; the sheep, hogs, fowl, and milch cows; the springhouse crocks of pickled beets and sauerkraut; the dried food and the seed bags and the spice racks that hung from nails hammered into the newspaper-covered walls of the main house. The material aspects of their surroundings represented fully the fabric of life as it had been known in the hundreds of abandoned cabins and barns and outbuildings that dotted the landscape of the Great Smoky Mountains National Park. And the Walker sisters were not about to give up their way of life without a struggle. In a poem, "My Mountain Home," Louisa expressed the family's feelings:

"There is an old weather bettion house
That stands near a wood
With an orchard near by it
For all most one hundred years it has stood

"It was my home in infency
It sheltered me in youth
When I tell you I love it
I tell you the truth

"For years it has sheltered
By day and night
From the summer sun's heat
And the cold winter blight.

"But now the park commesser
Comes all dressed up so gay
Saying this old house of yours
We must now take away

Little Greenbrier Cove was known to some people as Five Sisters Cove because of the Walker sisters' place just above the schoolhouse. The Walkers had their garden and grape arbors close to the house for handy tending.

Inside, everything was neat as a pin with coats, hats, baskets, guns, and what-have-you hanging on the newspaper-covered walls.

Sitting on the front porch are (from left) Polly, Louisa, and Martha. Also on the porch is a loom made by their father (see page 120) and a spinning wheel.

Joseph S. Hall

"They coax they wheedle
They fret they bark
Saying we have to have this place
For a National park

"For us poor mountain people
They dont have a care
But must a home for
The wolf the lion and the bear

"But many of us have a title
That is sure and will hold
To the City of peace
Where the streets are pure gold

"There no lion in its fury
Those pathes ever trod
It is the home of the soul
In the presence of God

"When we reach the portles
Of glory so fair
The Wolf cannot enter
Neather the lion or bear

"And no park Commissioner
Will ever dar
To desturbe or molest
Or take our home from us there."

Before leaving for Lufty Baptist Church, Alfred Dowdle and his family of Collins Creek pose for Joseph S. Hall, who was studying linguistics in the Smokies for the Park Service.

In January of 1941, however, the Walker sisters relented a little and sold their 50 hectares (123 acres) to the United States for $4,750 and a lifetime lease. Partly because of this unique situation, this special lifestyle, park officials delayed any well-defined program to recreate and present a vanishing culture. When the *Saturday Evening Post* "discovered" the Walker sisters in 1946, tourists in the Smokies flocked to the Walker home as if it were a museum of Appalachia. The sisters themselves tolerated the visitors, even sold mountain "souvenirs." But the years passed, three of the sisters died, and in 1953 Margaret Jane and Louisa wrote to the park superintendent:
"I have a request to you Will you please have the Sign a bout the Walker Sisters taken down the one on High Way 73 especially the reason I am asking

this there is just 2 of the sister lives at the old House place one is 70 years of age the other is 82 years of age and we can't receive so many visitors. We are not able to do our Work and receive so many visitors, and can't make sovioners to sell like we once did and people will be expecting us to have them...."

The park, of course, cooperated and helped the sisters until Louisa, the last, died in 1964.

Increasingly the park recognized the value of the human history of the Smokies. Out of that recognition came interpretive projects and exhibits at Cades Cove, Oconaluftee, Sugarlands, and a variety of other sites which showed and still show the resiliency and the creativity of the Appalachian mountaineer.

The same mix of problem, potential, and progress has made itself felt on the Eastern Band of the Cherokees. Their population within the Qualla Boundary doubled from approximately 2,000 in 1930 to more than 4,000 forty years later. This increase has only pointed more urgently to the economic, social, and cultural challenges confronting the Cherokees.

By 1930, the inhabitants of the Qualla Boundary had reached a kind of balance between the customs of the past and the demands of the present. Most families owned 12 or 16 hectares (30 or 40 acres) of woodland, with a sixth of that cleared and planted in corn, beans, or potatoes. A log or frame house, a small barn and other outbuildings, and the animals— a horse, a cow, a few hogs, chickens—rounded out the Cherokee family's possessions, which about equalled those of the neighboring whites. The Eastern Band itself was unified by two main strands: first, the land tenure system by which the more than 20,230 Qualla hectares (50,000 acres) could be leased, but not sold, to whites; and second, the lingering social organization of the clan.

These clans, which largely paralleled the five main towns of Birdtown, Wolftown, Painttown, Yellow Hill, and Big Cove, stabilized the population into groups and offered, through such methods as the dance, an outlet for communication and expression. Through the Friendship dance, for example, young people could meet each other. The Bugah dance depended upon joking and teasing among relatives. And the revered Eagle dance celebrated victory in

the ball games between Cherokee communities.

The whirlwind changes of the mid-20th century tipped whatever balance the Cherokees had gained. The Great Depression, World War II, and the explosion of tourism and mobility and business opportunity brought inside the Qualla Boundary both a schedule of modernization and a table of uncertainty. The dance declined in importance. Surrounding counties seemed to take better advantage of the new trends than these natives who had been cast into a political no-man's-land.

By the 1950s, the Eastern Band could look forward to a series of familiar paradoxes: relatively poor education; a wealth of small tourist enterprise and a dearth of large, stable industry; an unsurpassed mountain environment and an appalling state of public health. A 1955 survey of health conditions, for instance, found that 90 percent of 600 homes in seven Cherokee districts had insufficient water, sewage, and garbage facilities. More than 95 percent of the housing was substandard. Diseases springing from inadequate sanitation prevailed.

The situation changed and is still in the process of change. The Eastern Band could not and cannot allow such oversight, such undercommittment. The Qualla Boundary Community Action Program sponsored day-care centers in several Cherokee communities. In the years surrounding 1960, three industries manufacturing products from quilts to moccasins located at Cherokee and began to employ hundreds of men and women on a continuing, secure basis. A few years later, community action turned its efforts to the housing problem; as the program drove ahead, 400 homes were either "constructed or significantly improved," reducing the percentage of substandard houses to about 50 percent. As for living facilities, the percentages have been exactly reversed: 90 percent of homes now have septic tanks and safe water.

The Cherokee Boys' Club, a nonprofit organization incorporated in 1964, has improved the quality of life within the Qualla Boundary. The club's self-supporting projects include a complete bus service for Cherokee schools and garbage collection for the North Carolina side of the Smokies. Along with the Qualla Civic Center, the Boys' Club serves a useful socializing function as the modern equivalent to past dances and rituals.

Dances are associated with certain traditional Cherokee games. Separate groups of women and lacrosse-like players are about to begin a pre-game dance in 1888.

Nine men celebrate a game victory with an Eagle Dance in 1932.

Samson Welsh shoots arrows with a blow gun at the Cherokee Indian Fair in 1936.

Perhaps the soundest of the native Cherokee businesses is the Qualla Arts and Crafts Mutual. Since 1947, the Qualla Co-op has marketed the work of hundreds of Indian craftsmen. Magnificent carvings of cherry and walnut and baskets of river cane and honeysuckle preserve the skills and art of the past and symbolize the performance and the promise of the Eastern Band of the Cherokees.

The Tennessee portion of the Great Smoky Mountains has seen its share of major accomplishments through imagination and hard work. One such accomplishment is Gatlinburg's Arrowmont School of Arts and Crafts, known as the Pi Beta Phi Settlement School during the early years of the century.

In 1910, Gatlinburg comprised a half-dozen houses, a couple of general stores, a church, and scant educational facilities. Perhaps 200 families lived in the upper watershed of the Little Pigeon River, and these families looked to Gatlinburg for trading, visiting, and whatever learning they could reasonably expect to receive during their lifetimes. In that year, the national sorority of Pi Beta Phi decided to establish a needed educational project somewhere in rural America; after discussing a possible site with the U.S. commissioner of education, who suggested Tennessee, and the state commissioner, who chose Sevier County, and the county superintendent, who pointed to the isolated community of Gatlinburg, the group picked this little village in the shadow of the Great Smokies as the area in which they would work.

On February 20, 1912, Martha Hill, a neatly dressed and determined young brunette from Nashville, opened school in an abandoned Baptist church at the junction of Baskins Creek and the Little Pigeon River. Thirteen suspicious but willing pupils, their ages ranging from 4 to 24, offered themselves for instruction. At first, attendance was irregular, but by Christmastime, a celebration at the schoolroom drew a crowd of 300. Miss Hill, herself tired and a bit ill from spending exhausting hours nursing several sick neighbors, had to be brought to the party by wagon from a cottage she had leased for $1.50 per month.

The winter warmed into spring and the one-room school grew into a settlement school. Workers from Pi Beta Phi organized a sewing club for girls, a baseball club for boys. Martha Hill gathered some books together to form the nucleus of a library. Students built barns and chicken houses on land bought with sorority and community contributions.

During the next two years, achievements small and large piled upon each other. The library expanded to almost 2,000 books; school enrollment swelled to well over 100. Pi Phi sank a second well, tended a fruit orchard, took the children on their first trip to Maryville. The people of Gatlinburg began to accept the school both in spirit and in fact.

Activities branched out into other fields. In the fall of 1920, nurse Phyllis Higinbotham, an experienced graduate of Johns Hopkins, converted the old cottage into a hospital. Endowed with both unswerving dedication and unending friendliness, "Miss Phyllis" walked and rode from house to house, trained midwives, taught hygiene, and persuaded doctors from Knoxville and Sevierville to keep occasional office hours in Gatlinburg. In 1926, after firmly establishing a model rural health center, Phyllis Higinbotham became state supervisor of public health nurses for Tennessee.

As time passed, the county and the burgeoning town assumed greater responsibility for the Pi Beta Phi Settlement School's crucial progress in the vital areas of health and education. But the broad-based school was by no means undermined. Almost as soon as it had arrived in Gatlinburg, Pi Phi had begun offering adult courses in home economics, agriculture, weaving, and furniture making. These courses formed the basis for a true cottage industry which in the late 1920s benefitted more than 100 local families. And when the coming of the Great Smoky Mountains National Park assured a constant wave of tourism, the products of folk culture in the Smokies rode the crest of that wave.

The present-day Arrowmont School of Arts and Crafts, located upon a peaceful estate in the heart of commercial Gatlinburg, attests to the imagination of a generous group, the cooperation of a chosen community, and the lasting good works of both. Like Qualla, like the CCC camps, like the park today, and, most of all, like the Walker place, Arrowmont signifies the profound beauty that can result when people practice a simple respect for their homeland.

Handicrafts

Woods and meadows, fields and meadows, fields and mines and swamps, every part of the natural scene yielded some material that could be transformed into a handcrafted article of usefulness and beauty. From the trees came richly grained lumber for furniture and musical instruments, sturdy timber for tools and utensils, and softer wood for whittling "play-pretties" and purely decorative cbjects. Wood-working, even sculpture, became one of the outstanding skills of mountain artisans. All the crafts involved in textile de-

Laura Thornborough

sign and production were part of the region's history: weaving and spinning, quilting and braiding and hooking, making dyes from roots, barks, vegetables, herbs. Baskets were woven from oak and hickory splits, from river cane, and honeysuckle vines. Cherokee and mountaineer alike shared designs and shapes for the baskets made from different materials for uses ranging from egg-gathering to household storage. And, as illustrated by Mrs. Matt Ownby (left) and Mack McCarter (below), basket-

Alan Rinehart

making was something done by both men and women. Clay, fashioned on rude, homemade potter's wheels of the earlier days, provided pots and pitchers of primitive handsomeness and daily utility. Broomcorn and sedge offered materials for rough but effective brooms. Leather crafts arose from the need for harnesses on mules and horse, and shoes on people. Skinning, treating, tanning were just the first steps of a long, demanding process of turning raw hide into usable leather. The use of corn shucks illustrated with special clarity the mountain person's inventiveness in utilizing everything he raised or acquired. Corn shucks could make a stout chair-bottom or a captivating little mountain doll. Nimble fingers turned the husks into a dozen different articles. In his *Handicrafts of the Southern Highlands,* Allen H. Eaton wrote in 1937: "We must try to find the qualities of excellence which these people have developed before insisting that they accept our formula for living, thinking, and expression. . . .

Better certainly, if we know, as those who have worked and lived in the Highlands have had a chance to know, what are the standards and the ideals to which the people cling. But even that experience should not be necessary for us to understand and to cherish the spirit of the young highlander who, after expressing gratitude to the missionary who had come in to help build a school, said with characteristic mountain frankness, 'Bring us your civilization, but leave us our own culture.' "

Claude Huskey and Mack McCarter make chairs at one of the shops in Gatlinburg in the 1930s.

John Jones was the miller in the late 1930s at the Mingus Creek Mill in Oconaluftee.

Tom and Jerry Hearon, along with John Burns, hew a log trough with a broad ax and adze.

With a mallet and ax, Tom and Jerry Hearon split logs into bolts from which to make shingles.

Dave Bohanan feeds cane between the rollers as he makes sorghum molasses.

A Smokies resident builds a flat bed for his sourwood sled.

Coming Home

Tremont. This Tennessee valley of the Middle Prong of the Little River does not differ widely from Deep Creek or Greenbrier or Cosby or most of the other branches and hollows of the Smokies. Each, including Tremont, penetrates the hills, divides them like a furrow, and protects its own rocky, racing stream with a matting of thick, green growth. Nearby Cades Cove and North Carolina's Cataloochee might guard a few hectares of lush, hill-cradled pasture or farmland, but even these are stamped with the clear, cool air and feel of the Great Smoky Mountains.

A visit to the cabin of John and Lurena Oliver takes a family back to yesteryear in Cades Cove.

So Tremont is representative. And, perhaps because of this, it is a symbol—a symbol of both the mystery and the clarity of the mountains which give it a name. There is, for example, the legend of a small boy who wandered into the backcountry above the "Sinks" and was lost for two days. Uncle Henry Stinnett, a worried neighbor, searched in vain for the boy until he dreamed, on the second night, of a child sleeping near a log on a familiar ridge. Henry Stinnett renewed the search, and the boy was indeed found asleep "under the uprooted stump of a tree."

And side by side with such a strange vision exists its opposite: the unforeseen. In August of 1947, a young woman was sunbathing on the boulders of the river. While she enjoyed the rays of the warm sun downstream, the high upper reaches of the prong were being flooded by the swollen, flash attacks of a hidden cloudburst. Within minutes, the woman drowned in a hurtling wall of water.

Yet there is also a clarity here that offsets the unknown. It is a quality of outlook, a confidence of ability and expectation for the future as immense as the mountains which inspire it. But it is an awareness grounded in the facts of history and anecdote and the crisp, fresh sounds of children's voices.

"Black Bill" Walker knew about children; he had more than 25 himself. A double first cousin to the father of Little Greenbrier's Walker sisters, "Black Bill" or "Big Will" Walker moved into the lonely valley in 1859. He was only 21 years old then, and his name was simply William. He was accompanied by his strong 19-year-old wife, Nancy.

His mother was a Scot, a member of the McGill clan. His father, Marion, was another of those multi-talented frontiersmen: miller, cattleman, orchardist, bear hunter, saddlebag preacher. William took up

Fred R. Bell

where his parents left off. He became the leader, the ruler of the community he had started. He was rumored to have been a Mormon, although denominations mattered little in the wilderness. He and Nancy raised seven children. Later wives bore him approximately 20 more.

He milled his own corn and built log cabins for each of his families. He fashioned an immense muzzle-loading rifle, nicknamed it "Old Death," and handled it with rare skill. Horace Kephart, in a 1918 magazine article, tells of a conversation he had with the 80-year-old hunter:

"Black Bill's rifle was one he made with his own hands in the log house where I visited him. He rifled it on a wooden machine that was likewise of his own make, and stocked it with wood cut on his own land. The piece was of a little more than half-ounce bore, and weighed 12½ pounds . . . the old hunter showed me how he loaded. . . .

" 'My bullets are run small enough so that a naked one will jest slip down on the powder by its own weight. When I'm in a hurry, I pour in the powder by guess, wet a bullet in my mouth, and drop it down the gun. Enough powder sticks to it to keep the ball from falling out if I shoot downhill. Then I snatch a cap from one o' these strings, and—so.'

"The old man went through the motions like a sleight-of-hand performer. The whole operation of loading took barely ten seconds."

After Black Bill's own children had grown, he went to the nearby town of Maryville and requested and received a school in the valley for children yet to come. He governed his settlement, yet he was not merely a governor. He was a remarkable man, an individualist who also built a community.

After Black Bill's death in 1919, life in Tremont continued as before. Families still ate turkey and pheasant, squirrel and venison, sweet potatoes and the first greenery of spring, onions. Children's bare feet remained tough enough to break open chestnut burrs. Mothers continued to put dried peaches in a jar full of moonshine, let it sit a day or two, and test their peach brandy with a sip or two. And on Christmas, fathers and sons "got out and shot their guns" in celebration.

Intervals of violence interrupted the daily routine. Farmers with cattle and sheep freely roaming the

"It is point blank aggravating; I can't walk a log like I used to," Aden Carver told H. C. Wilburn as he crossed Bradley Fork in October 1937 at the age of 91.

ridges sometimes made it hard for others to grow corn and similar crops. A hunter's bear and 'coon dogs might kill some sheep. One "war" ended with a fire on Fodder Stack Mountain that raced down into Chestnut Flats and killed a number of sheep. No humans died, but the sheep men killed all the hunting dogs in the vicinity.

By the early 1920s, change was creeping into the valley. The Little River Lumber Company persuaded Black Bill's children to do what he would not do: sell the timber. From the mid-twenties to the mid-thirties, more than 1,000 workers lived in the logging town of Tremont, patronized the Tremont Hotel, and hauled away tens of thousands of the virgin forest's giants.

With the Great Smoky Mountains National Park came the CCC. The Civilian Conservation Corps camp on the old lumber site, together with a Girl Scout camp that would last until 1959, signaled a retreat—and a progression—from the extractive industry of the past. Although the CCC disbanded during World War II, a modern-day CCC arrived in 1964. The Job Corps combined conservation work, such as trail maintenance and stream cleaning, with training in vital skills of roadbuilding, masonry, and the operation of heavy machinery.

Then, in 1969, Tremont entered a new era. The previous years of innovation seemed to prepare the secluded valley for a truly fresh and creative effort in education. The Walkers would have been proud of what came to be the Environmental Education Center.

The Center draws on both original and time-tested techniques to teach grade school children basic awareness and respect for the natural world around them. Because its achievements are both fundamental and effective, and because it treats a splendid mountain area as a lasting and deserving homeland for plants and animals and human beings, the story of Tremont culminates this history of the Great Smoky Mountains. For here is one of the ways the Smokies can be best used: as a wild refuge and a living laboratory where young people may discover the deeper meaning of the park's past and why, for the future, there is a park at all.

The Environmental Education Center, administered by Maryville College from 1969 through 1979 and since then by Great Smoky Mountains Natural History Association, evolved through planning by both the park and nearby county school systems. One of the rangers, Lloyd Foster, became so attached to the ideas being presented that he obtained a leave of absence from his work, persistently promoted the project, and became Tremont's first director. Experienced teachers such as Elsie Burrell and Randolph Shields helped Foster convert talk into action, rhetoric into experience.

The center soon offered a real alternative to conventional and overcrowded schools caught in the midst of industrialization. Teacher-led or parent-supervised classes from a multitude of states and cities organized themselves, paid a base fee for each member, and came to the valley for one week during the year. Within months, Tremont was teaching elementary students at the rate of thousands per year. The organizers retained their informal, camp-like approach to interested groups and added to the original dining room and two dormitories an audiovisual room and a laboratory complete with powerful microscopes. As the program expanded, children could fulfill their imaginative promptings in an art room, or build a miniature skidder in the crafts room, or turn to a library of extensive readings.

As the idea of environmental education at Tremont and elsewhere spread by word of mouth, volunteers from across the country arrived and aided those already at work. High school and college students participated in and still attend weekend conferences on the activities and the progress of the Center.

They learn, first of all, fundamental concepts that are expressed simply: "You don't have to have a lot of fancy buildings to do a good program," or "You know, sometimes we teach a lot of theory and we don't really get down to—I guess you'd call it the nitty-gritty," or even "Now don't chicken out, the way some of you did last time, step in the water."

They learn of "quiet hour," when, at the beginning of the week, each child stakes out a spot for himself in the woods, beside the stream, wherever choice leads. For an hour each day, in sun or rain, everybody seeks his or her own place and is assured of peace and privacy. A girl writes a poem to her parents; a fourth-grader contemplates on a rock by the water; and almost everyone who observes the quiet hour looks forward to it eagerly each day.

They learn about the highly effective lessons that

Fred R. Bell

In an attempt to capture the spirit of the old days, a family climbs about a Cades Cove barn.

Pages 142-143: Members of the Tilman Ownby family of Dudley Creek, near Gatlinburg, gather for a reunion in the early 1900s. Many of their descendants still live in the Smokies area today.

National Park Service

are scattered throughout the week, lessons such as "man and water," "stream ecology," "continuity and change." Imaginative gatherings become not the exception but the rule: "Sometimes we take a group of children, divide them into members of a make-believe pioneer family, and take them up into a wilderness area, an area which is truly pristine, almost a virgin forest. And we let the kids imagine that they are this pioneer family, and that they are going to pick out a house site." In one game called "succession," a boy from blacktopped, "civilized" Atlanta might search along a road for signs of life on the pavement, then in the gravel, then in the grass, then within the vast, teeming forest. And a day's trip to the Little Greenbrier schoolhouse gives the children of today a chance to experience what it was like when the Walker sisters and their ancestors sat on the hard wooden benches and learned the three R's and felt the bite of a hickory switch.

It may seem odd that modern children should enjoy so much a trip to school. But enjoy it they do, for as they fidget on the wooden benches or spell against each other in an old-fashioned "spelldown" or read a mid-1800s dictionary that defines a kiss as "a salute with the lips," they enter into a past place and a past time. For a few minutes, at least, they identify with the people who used to be here in these Smokies—not "play-acting" but struggling to survive and improve their lives.

The schoolhouse itself is old, built in 1882 out of poplar logs and white oak shingles. Its single room used to double as a church for the community, but now the two long, narrow windows on either side open out onto the protected forest of the park. A woman stands in the doorway, dressed in a pink bonnet and an old-fashioned, ankle-length dress. She rings a cast iron bell. The children, who have been out walking on this early spring morning, hear the bell and begin to run toward it. Some of them see the school and shout and beckon the others. In their hurry, they spread out and fill the clearing with flashes of color and expectation. The woman in the doorway is their teacher.

They have spanned a century and longer. They now live in more worlds than one, because they have come to the place where their spirit lives. It is again homecoming in the Great Smoky Mountains.

Children anxiously line up to go back a few years with Elsie Burrell at the one-room schoolhouse in Little Greenbrier.

Clair Burket

145

Part 3

Guide and Adviser

Traveling in the Smokies

"You can't get there from here," an oldtimer might tell you about traveling in the Smokies, and you might think that's true when you get on some of the back roads in the area. But if you stick mostly to the paved roads and use your auto map and the map in this book, you should not have much or any trouble finding your way around Great Smoky Mountains National Park.

The park, which is administered by the National Park Service, U.S. Department of the Interior, is located along the border between North Carolina and Tennessee. It can be reached by major highways in both states and by the Blue Ridge Parkway, which connects the park with Shenandoah National Park in Virginia. Newfound Gap Road, the only road that crosses the park, connects Gatlinburg, Tennessee, with Cherokee, North Carolina. It is closed to commercial vehicles.

There are just a few other roads within the park itself, so travel between distant points is quite roundabout and time consuming. But you will see plenty of nice scenery along the way. Because this handbook focuses on the history of the area, the travel information does, too. But by no means should you let the limited scope presented here limit what you do. We encourage you to enjoy the scenic views, flowers, shrubs, and wildlife as you travel to and through the historic sites. For example, while you're in the Cable Mill area at Cades Cove, you might take the trail to Abrams Falls. It's a delightful short hike to a beautiful spot in the park. And if you take the Roaring Fork Auto Tour, you might hike the 2.4 kilometers (1.5 miles) through a hemlock forest to Grotto Falls. There are plenty of other short hikes in the park, and when you take them you may come across decaying ruins of early settlements.

Visitor Centers

Park headquarters and the major visitor center are at Sugarlands, 3.2 kilometers (2 miles) south of Gatlinburg. Other visitor centers are at Cades Cove and at Oconaluftee, both of which are prime historical areas in the park. The Sugarlands and Oconaluftee centers are open 8 a.m. to 4:30 p.m. during the winter, with extended hours the rest of the year. The Cades Cove center, located in the Cable Mill area on the loop road, is open from 9 a.m. to 5 p.m. from mid-April through October. Exhibits at the Cades Cove and Oconaluftee centers feature the human history of the Smokies. The relative flatness of the Cades Cove area makes this the best place to bicycle in the park.

Walks and Talks

Some of the guided walks and evening programs deal with history. Check schedules at the visitor centers and campgrounds or in the park newspaper.

Mountain lifeways and skills are demonstrated periodically from early spring through October at the Pioneer Farmstead at Oconaluftee, Cades Cove, Mingus Mill, and Little Greenbrier School. At Oconaluftee you can walk through a typical Smokies farm and see many of yesteryear's household chores being demonstrated. At Cades Cove, you can see, among other things, how sorghum and wooden shingles were made. Millers seasonally operate the gristmills near Oconaluftee and at Cades Cove. All of these demonstrations indicate that the good old days were not easy ones.

Further Information

For more detailed travel and natural history information, see Handbook 112, *Great Smoky Mountains,* in this National Park Service series. This book and an extensive array of literature about various aspects of the park are sold at the Sugarlands, Oconaluftee, and Cades Cove visitor centers by a nonprofit organization that assists the park's interpretive programs. For a price list, write to: Great Smoky Mountains Natural History Association, Gatlinburg, TN 37738.

Specific questions can be addressed to: Superintendent, Great Smoky Mountains National Park, Gatlinburg, TN 37738. The headquarters' telephone number is (615) 436-5615.

Accommodations and Services

You can obtain gasoline, food, lodging, and camping supplies in most communities near the park in both Tennessee and North Carolina. Several campgrounds are located in both the park and in the nearby towns.

Within the park, only LeConte Lodge and Wonderland Hotel offer accommodations, and they are limited. A half-day hike up a mountain trail is required to reach LeConte Lodge, which is open from mid-April to late October. Rustic hotel accommodations and food service are provided at Wonderland Hotel in Elkmont from June 1 to October 1.

Write to the chambers of commerce in the communities near the park for general travel advice and for current information on the availability of lodging facilities.

Safety

While touring the park's historical sites, stay on the trails, keep children under control, enjoy the farm animals at a distance, and stay safely away from the millwheels and other machinery.

While traveling throughout the park, beware of the many black bears no matter how tame they may appear. If they approach your vehicle, keep the windows closed. Do not feed the bears!

And keep in mind that the weather can change quickly in the Smokies and that hypothermia can strike not only in the winter but at any season. Be careful not to become wet and/or chilled. Carry extra clothing.

See Handbook 112, *Great Smoky Mountains*, for more precautions and information about the black bear, hypothermia, and other dangers.

Regulations

Roads within the park are designed for scenic driving, so stay within the speed limits and be alert for slow vehicles and for others exiting and entering. Pull off the roads or park only at designated areas. Gasoline is not sold in the park, so be sure to fill your tank before heading on a long trip.

Do not leave valuables inside a locked car where they can be seen. Leave them home, take them with you when you leave your vehicle, or lock them in the trunk.

Hunting is prohibited in the park. Firearms must be broken down so they cannot be used. The use of archery equipment, game calls, and spotlights also is prohibited.

All plants, animals, and artifacts are protected by Federal law here. Do not disturb them in any way. Fishing is permitted subject to state and Federal regulations and licensing.

All overnight camping in the backcountry requires a backcountry permit. Otherwise, camp and build fires only in designated campground sites.

We suggest that you do not bring pets. They are permitted in the park but only if on a leash or under other physical control. They may not be taken on trails or cross-country hikes. Veterinary services are found nearby. If you want to board your pet during your stay here, check with the nearby chambers of commerce.

Oconaluftee

Self-sufficiency and individuality were strong traits in the Smokies. Each person had to do a variety of tasks, and each family member had to help or complement the others. Just as Milas Messer (see pages 90-91) exemplified these traits personally, the Pioneer Farmstead at Oconaluftee on the North Carolina side of the park represents them structurally. Various buildings have been brought here to create a typical Smokies farmstead on the banks of the Oconaluftee River.

In the summer and fall farm animals roam about the farmstead and a man and a woman carry out daily chores to give you an idea of what the pioneers had to do just to exist. At first these Jacks- and Jills-of-all-trades had no stores to go to. They made their own tools, built their own houses and barns and outbuildings, raised their own food, made their own clothes, and doctored themselves, for the most part.

The log house here is a particularly nice one, for John Davis built it with matched walls. He split the logs in half and used the halves on opposite walls. The two stone chimneys are typical of the earliest houses. Davis' sons, then 8 and 4, collected rocks for the chimneys with oxen and a sled.

Behind the house is an essential building, the meathouse. Here meat, mostly pork, was layered on the shelf at the far end and covered with a thick coating of salt. After the meat had cured, it was hung from poles, which go from end to end, to protect it from rodents. In the early years especially, bear meat and venison hung alongside the pork.

Apples were a big part of the settlers' diet in a variety of forms: cider, vinegar, brandy, sauces, and pies. And of course they ate them, too, right off the tree. The thick rock walls on the

At the Pioneer Farmstead in Oconaluftee you can get a glimpse of what daily farm life was like in the Smokies. Besides the ongoing kitchen tasks, chores included tending cows and chickens, cutting and stacking hay, building and repairing barns and wagons, and a thousand other things.

150

lower floor of the apple house protect the fruit from freezing in winter. The summer apples were kept on the log-wall second floor.

The Indians' maize, or corn, was the most essential crop on the typical Smokies farmstead. Besides being used as food for livestock, it was the staple for the pioneers themselves. With corn they made corn bread, hoe cakes, corn meal mush, and even a little moon-shine. The harvested crop was kept dry in a corncrib until used.

As the pioneers became more set-tled and turned into farmers, they built barns to provide shelter for their cows, oxen, sheep, and horses, plus some of their farming equipment and hay. The large, log barn at the Oconaluftee Farmstead is unusual. It is a drovers' barn—a hotel for cattle and other ani-mals driven to market. The barn is located close to its original site.

Most farmers had a small black-smith shop where they could bang out a few tools, horseshoes, hinges, and, later on, parts for farm machinery. These structures were not very sophisticated; they just had to provide a little shelter so the fire could be kept going and to protect the equipment— and to keep the smith dry—during inclement weather.

The springhouse served not only as the source of water but as a refrig-erator. Here milk, melons, and other foods were kept, many of them in large crocks. The water usually ran through the springhouse in one half of a hollowed out log, or in a rock-lined trench. On hot, muggy days, a child sent to the springhouse for food or water might tarry a moment or two to enjoy the air conditioning.

The farmstead is open all year, but the house is open only from May to November.

Cades Cove

Just as Oconaluftee represents self-sufficiency and individuality, Cades Cove illustrates those traits, plus something else: a sense of community. Here individuals and families worked hard at eking out a living from day to day, but here, too, everyone gathered together from time to time to help harvest a crop, raise a barn, build a church, and maintain a school. The structural evidence of this helping-hand attitude still stands today in Cataloochee (see pages 154-155) and in Cades Cove.

At its peak in 1850, Cades Cove had 685 residents in 132 households. A few years after that the population shrank to 275 as the soil became overworked and as new lands opened up in the West. Then the population rose again to about 500 just before the park was established.

The State of Tennessee had acquired this land in 1820 from the Cherokees and then sold it to speculators, who in turn sold plots to the settlers. They cleared most of the trees and built their houses at the foot of the surrounding hills. Corn, wheat, oats, and rye were raised on the flat lands, whereas the slopes were used for pastures, orchards, and vegetable gardens. The Park Service leases some of the land here today to farmers to keep the cove open as it was in the early settlement days.

In Cades Cove you will find some of the finest log buildings in America. Some are original; the others come from elsewhere in the park. The first log house on the 18-kilometer (11-mile)-loop-road tour belonged to John and Lurena Oliver, who bought their land in 1826. Their cabin, with its stone chimney and small windows, is typical of many in the Smokies, and it remained in the Oliver family until the

The Methodist Church, Cable Mill, and Gregg-Cable house are just three of the many log or frame structures still standing in Cades Cove today.

park was established. A stone in the Primitive Baptist Church cemetery just down the road commemorates John and Lurena, the first permanent white settlers in the cove. The church was organized in 1827, and the log building was used until 1887, though the members, who were pro-Union, felt they had to shut it down during the Civil War because of strong rebel sentiment.

The Methodist Church supposedly was built by one man, J. D. McCampbell, in 115 days for $115, and after he was done he served as its preacher for many years. The frame Missionary Baptist Church was built in 1894 by a group that split from the Primitive Baptists in 1839 because it endorsed missionary work.

Elijah Oliver's log house may well be one of the first split-levels. The lower kitchen section off the back formerly was the home of the Herron family and was brought here and attached to the main house. This is a good place to see some of the many auxiliary structures most families had: springhouse, barn, and smokehouse.

Many families also had a tub mill with which they could grind a bushel of corn a day. When they had more corn to grind, they would take it to a larger mill, such as John Cable's. His was not the first waterwheel mill in Cades Cove, but it is the only remaining one today. It has been rehabilitated a few times, but the main framing, the millstones, and some of the gears are original.

In the Cable Mill area are several other structures that have been brought here from other parts of the park. Among them is the Gregg-Cable house, possibly the first frame house in Cades Cove. It was built by Leason Gregg in 1879 and later became the home, until her death in 1940, of Becky Cable, John's daughter. At different times the house served as a store and a boarding-house. The blacksmith shop, barns, smokehouse, corncrib, and sorghum mill are representative of such structures in the Smokies.

Heading east from the mill area, you come to the Henry Whitehead and Dan Lawson places. At both you can see some of the best log work, inside and out, within the park, and both have brick instead of stone chimneys. These houses represent the transition between the crude log house and the finer log house. Further down the road is "Hamp" Tipton's place, where you can see an apiary or bee gum stand. Honey, sorghum, and maple syrup were common sweets for folks in the Cove.

The last house on the loop road is the Carter Shields place, a one-story log house with loft. This cabin is about the average size of Smokies cabins, but it is a bit fancier than most with its beaded paneling in the living room and a closed-in stairway.

The buildings in Cades Cove are open all year except for the churches and a few other structures.

Other Historic Sites in the Park

Cades Cove and Oconaluftee are the primary locations of historic structures in the national park, but elsewhere there are a few interesting buildings to see.

From Gatlinburg head south on Airport Road, which runs into Cherokee Orchard Road in the park. Soon you come to Noah "Bud" Ogle's place. Ogle and his wife, Cindy, started farming here on 160 hectares (400 acres) in 1879. Here you can see a log house, log barn, and restored tub mill.

South of the Ogle place you come to Roaring Fork Auto Tour. On this one-way 8-kilometer (5-mile) tour you can see that nature has reclaimed most of the Roaring Fork community. Among the few remaining buildings are Jim Bales' corncrib and barn, plus a log house that was moved here.

Home for Ephraim Bales, his wife, and nine children consisted of two joined log cabins. The smaller one was the kitchen, and in front of its hearth is a "tater hole." Family members could lift up a floor board, remove some potatoes from storage, and toss them on the fire to bake. Other structures here include a corncrib and barn.

A log house and mill are the only structures that remain of the many that belonged to Alfred Reagan, one of Roaring Fork's more talented residents. He was a farmer, blacksmith, preacher, miller, storekeeper, and carpenter. His house was more refined than most in the Smokies.

The Roaring Fork Auto Tour road is open from mid-April to mid-November.

In the Oconaluftee Valley just north of the Pioneer Farmstead is Mingus Mill, built for Abraham Mingus in the 1870s by Sion Thomas Early. This gristmill, the finest and most advanced in the Smokies, has a water-powered turbine beneath it. Water flows down a

On the way to and from Sugar-lands you can take side trips to (below) Mingus Mill, Little Greenbrier School, and Bud Ogle's place at Roaring Fork. Plan on devoting nearly a full day to visit isolated Cataloo-chee, where you can see (right) the Caldwell home, school-house, Palmer Chapel, and several other structures.

National Park Service

154

millrace and flume to the mill, and, when the flume gate is raised, fills the penstock to power the turbine. The mill has two sets of grinding stones, one for corn and one for wheat. The mill was in operation until 1936, reopened for a few months in 1940, and reconditioned by the Great Smoky Mountains Natural History Association in 1968. It is open daily from May through October with a miller usually on duty to explain its workings.

North of Mingus Mill is Smokemont. All that remains of this small community is the Oconaluftee Baptist Church, a frame structure that sits high on a bluff.

Just off Little River Road between Sugarlands and Tremont is Little Greenbrier School (see pages 85 and 144). In the summer an interpreter often is on hand to help children, and adults, understand what going to school was like in the Smokies. The road to the school is narrow and unpaved and not the easiest to negotiate in inclement weather, so you may want to walk in.

Several buildings are still standing in the isolated Cataloochee area on the North Carolina side of the park. They include Palmer Chapel, Beech Grove School, and the Jarvis Palmer, Hiram Caldwell, and Steve Woody homes. Most of the buildings are open, and a ranger is on duty to answer your questions. The fields are mowed to maintain the cove effect from early settlement days. Reaching Cataloochee from the north means a lengthy trip on unpaved road; from the south it's a bit easier. If you have the time, visiting Cataloochee is worth the extra effort.

Related Nearby Sites

A number of nearby sites are related in one way or the other to the history of the Great Smoky Mountains. Here are a few that you might visit while vacationing in the Smokies:

The arts, crafts, and lifeways of the Cherokees are portrayed by the tribe at the Qualla Reservation, adjacent to the North Carolina side of the park. The Museum of the Cherokee Indian displays a collection of artifacts, and the Oconaluftee Living Indian Village shows typical early Cherokee life in log structures. The play "Unto These Hills" tells the story of the Cherokees and their encounters with Europeans settling in the Smokies and of the forced removal of most of the tribe to Oklahoma in 1838. About 4,000 Cherokees live on the Qualla Reservation today.

The Arrowmont School of Arts and Crafts in Gatlinburg has done much to perpetuate the pottery, weaving, and other skills indicative of the Smokies people. The school displays and sells objects created by local artisans.

The Museum of Appalachia in Norris, Tennessee, just north of Knoxville, has 30 restored pioneer log structures, a representative farmstead, and more than 200,000 artifacts of mountain life.

The Blue Ridge Parkway, administered by the National Park Service, has several log houses, a gristmill, a reconstructed farm, and other early American buildings. Much of the 755-kilometer (469-mile), parkway, which adjoins Great Smoky Mountains National Park near Oconaluftee and runs north into Virginia, is quite far from the park, but some of the historic points of interest are in the southern portion. The Folk Art Center, at milepost 382, displays traditional crafts of the Southern Highlands.

At Mabry Mill on the Blue Ridge Parkway you can see old-time skills demonstrated in the summer and fall. Weaving is just one of many traditional crafts taught at the Arrowmont School of Arts and Crafts in Gatlinburg.

Armchair Explorations

General histories of the Great Smoky Mountains:

Elizabeth Skaggs Bowman, *Land of High Horizons,* 1938

Carlos C. Campbell, *Birth of a National Park,* 1960

Michael Frome, *Strangers in High Places,* 1980

Horace Kephart, *Our Southern Highlanders,* 1922

Horace Kephart, *Journals* at Western Carolina University

Robert Lindsay Mason, *The Lure of the Great Smokies,* 1927

Roderick Peattie, ed., *The Great Smokies and the Blue Ridge,* 1943

Laura Thornborough, *The Great Smoky Mountains,* 1937

Cherokee history:

James Adair, *The History of the American Indians,* 1775

William Bartram, *Travels,* 1792

John P. Brown, *Old Frontiers,* 1938

William H. Gilbert, *The Eastern Cherokees,* 1943

Henry T. Malone, *Cherokees of the Old South,* 1956

James Mooney, *Myths of the Cherokees,* 1900

Charles C. Royce, *The Cherokee Nation of Indians,* 1887

William L. Smith, *The Story of the Cherokees,* 1927

Henry Timberlake, *Memoirs,* 1765

Grace Steele Woodward, *The Cherokees,* 1963

Other historical works:

W. C. Allen, *The Annals of Haywood County,* 1935

John Preston Arthur, *Western North Carolina,* 1914

John C. Campbell, *The Southern Highlander and His Homeland,* 1921

Wilma Dykeman, *The French Broad,* 1955

Allen H. Eaton, *Handicrafts of the Southern Highlands,* 1937

Paul Fink, "Early Explorers in the Great Smokies," *East Tennessee Historical Society Bulletin,* 1933

Joseph S. Hall, *Smoky Mountain Folks and Their Lore,* 1960

Joseph S. Hall, *Yarns and Tales from the Great Smokies,* 1978

Archibald Henderson, *The Conquest of the Old Southwest,* 1920

Charles Lanman, *Letters from the Alleghany Mountains,* 1849

Ruth W. O'Dell, *Over the Misty Blue Hills: The Story of Cocke County, Tennessee,* 1950

John Parris, articles in *The Asheville Citizen-Times*

Randolph Shields, "Cades Cove," *Tennessee Historical Quarterly,* 1965

Randolph Shields, *The Cades Cove Story,* 1977

Foster A. Sondley, *A History of Buncombe County,* 1930

Wilbur Zeigler and Ben Grosscup, *The Heart of the Alleghanies,* 1883

Robert Woody, "Life on Little Cataloochee," *South Atlantic Quarterly,* 1950

157

Index

Numbers in italics refer to photographs, illustrations, or maps.

☆ GPO: 1984—421-611/10001

Handbook 125

The cover photograph was taken by Ed Cooper. The rest of the color photography, unless otherwise credited, was taken by William A. Bake of Boone, North Carolina. Nearly all of the black-and-white photographs come from the files of Great Smoky Mountains National Park. About half of them were taken in the 1930s for historic recording purposes by Edouard E. Exline and Charles S. Grossman on behalf of the National Park Service. Exline was a landscape architect with the Civilian Conservation Corps and a photographer by avocation. Grossman was a structural architect for the park who was in charge of the cultural preservation program.

The other photographers who have been identified are Laura Thornborough, who resided in the Smokies and wrote the book *The Great Smoky Mountains;* Joseph S. Hall, who has studied and written about linguistics of the Smokies since the 1930s; Harry M. Jennison, a research botanist from the University of Tennessee who worked in the park from 1935 to 1940; H.C. Wilburn, a CCC history technician who collected and purchased artifacts of mountain life; Maurice Sullivan, a CCC wildlife technician who subsequently became a Park Service naturalist; Alden Stevens, a museum specialist for the Park Service; Jim Shelton, husband of one of the Walker sisters, Sarah Caroline; George Masa, who established the Asheville Photo Service shortly after World War I; Burton Wolcott; and National Park Service photographers George A. Grant, Alan Rinehart, Fred R. Bell, M. Woodbridge Williams, and Clair Burket.

Many of the logging photographs were donated to the park by the Little River Lumber Company. Most of the photographs of Cherokees come from the National Anthropological Archives at the Smithsonian Institution; many of them were taken by James Mooney in the Smokies area in 1888.